THE

SEPARATION

OF

CHURCH & STATE

Has America Lost
Its Moral Compass?

by
Stephen Strehle

Huntington House Publishers

Huntington House Publishers
P.O. Box 53788
Lafayette, Louisiana 70505

PRINTED IN THE UNITED STATES OF AMERICA

Library of Congress Card Catalog Number
2001087285
ISBN 1-56384-185-1

[Dylan] entered a rigid, born-again Christian period. His music lost its spark and vitality.

Daily Press 22 August 1997

And that which you've given me today is worth more than I could pay/And no matter what they say I believe in you.

Bob Dylan's "I believe in You"
from *Slow Train Coming*

Dedication

To Susan, my beloved wife
Song of Songs 2:1, 2

Contents

Foreword

Dietrich Bonhoeffer was a deeply conflicted man in the midst of World War II. He was a German theologian who had preached simple, literal obedience to the words of Christ and yet found it difficult to "turn the other cheek" and ignore the evil around him. Did following the words of Christ lead to the sacrifice of others? Are Christians called to follow Christ at the expense of their fellow human beings? Bonhoeffer was distraught over the matter but decided in the end to give up whatever theory he possessed of absolute perfection in order to do what was right. He thought it best to surrender his self-righteous, law-abiding posture and risk involvement, even if it meant participation in a world tainted and depraved with iniquity. Hitler must be stopped. The evil must end, even if it meant joining the German Abwehr (resistance) in its attempt to assassinate the *Führer* and being hung by Himmler for his participation in the plot a few days before liberation.[1]

Political involvement has always presented the church with certain risks and temptations. The most literal reading of the New Testament provides little direction for political involvement and much caution against the church's entanglement with the world and its lusts. Those who interpret the New Testament in a literal way tend to separate themselves from the world and disparage the corrupting influence of its power. (The early church, the Anabaptists of the Reformation, and American Fundamentalists serve as good examples of this tendency.) Søren Kierkegaard also represents this tradition when he says:

> What Christianity needs is not suffocating protection of the State; no, it needs fresh air, it needs persecution. . . . The State only works disaster. . . . By its protection it smothers Christianity to death, as a fat lady with her corpus overlies her baby. And it teaches Christianity the most disgusting bad habits, as for example, under the name of Christianity to employ the power of the police.[2]

These words serve as a sober reminder to the church. They should cause deep conflict within any Christian who would venture into a world so filled with temptation. Kierkegaard's call to separate the church from the state speaks from true Christian passion and has much to recommend it.

However, one must discern the times. "To everything there is a season and a time for every activity under heaven" (Eccles. 3:1). The wisdom of heaven is not the same for all times and all seasons. There is a "time to tear apart and a time to mend together, a time to be silent and a time to speak, a time to love and a time to hate, a time for war and a time for peace" (Eccles. 3:7, 8). The wisdom of heaven does not seek war or peace but discerns the proper course of action under given circumstances. Its wisdom recognizes the many courses of action sanctioned by God and determines when to do what in accordance with one's station in life (*Sitz im Leben*). In nineteenth century Denmark, Kierkegaard's call for separation might have been the proper course of action. The Church, in his mind, had been corrupted by its connection with government, and no longer preached a passionate message of true discipleship. However, what is necessary for a dead, state-run church in the nineteenth century does not hold fast in twentieth century America, where secularity is permeating all aspects of our lives and corrupting the church. The call for the separation of church and state in our culture has become an attempt by secular, left-wing forces to rid society of religious people and their influence. This position has nothing to do with the historical concerns of the church and everything to do with erecting a wall that excludes one's opponents and their ideas from participation in the process. It is one thing for the church to leave society out of its own need for separation and another thing to be forced out by those of a different ideological agenda.

Of course, this wall might not matter if we lived in previous times when the government was smaller in size and did not extend its tentacles into most aspects of our lives. But today in America, where citizens spend an average of 40 percent of their income on taxes, (and the government continues to grow), it is difficult for the church to maintain a separate existence. The call for separation in this system becomes a means of relegating the church to the fringes of society, away from the center of power and changing all of us into a more worldly image through its power to transform the culture at large.[3] It becomes a means of teaching a most profane and sacrilegious doctrine—that religion is not essential to society and that one can create a society free from its passions—all one needs to do is identify it and eliminate it.

This book is dedicated to the destruction of this blasphemy. It believes that religious assumptions form an integral part of our nation's past and present-day existence. It believes that the separation of church and state is an incoherent device designed by those who wish to hide their own religious assumptions (pretending they are secular or neutral in this regard) and accent the more visible religious commitment of their opponents—all in an attempt to suppress them.

In a pluralistic society, one must treat all segments of the society in an equal manner when the government is involved, and it is unconscionable to dismiss certain people and their ideas from the process as second-class citizens unworthy of representation. Of course, one may wish to reduce the power of religion and ideological coercion in society, but the way to achieve this noble goal is through the reduction of the size of government, not through a ruse like church/state separation and the dismissal of certain elements from participation. This author believes that the government should practice vigilance to insure that its people are represented in accordance with their proportion in society. This book advocates a return to religious pluralism as the hallmark of a free society. It believes that no opinion should be condemned to silence. In fact, all must be heard in a debate to gain a sense of the issues at hand and develop a nuanced position in the end. It is only in the midst of a wide diversity of ideas that the truth will shine forth to those who seek it. This author believes that the wall of separation only exists to exclude certain segments of American society from exerting a meaningful influence upon the culture as a whole. Every brick of the wall must come tumbling down.

Stephen Strehle
St. Leo University
Hampton, VA

Notes

1. D. Bonhoeffer, *Ethics*, ed. E. Bethge (New York: The Macmillan Co., 1967), 240, 245, 260-261, 273.

2. S. Kierkegaard, *Attack upon "Christendom,"* trans. W. Lowrie (Princeton: Princeton University Press, 1972), 140.

3. M. McConnell, "Religious Freedom at a Crossroads," *The Bill of Rights in the Modern State*, ed. G. R. M. Stone, R. A. Epstein, and C. R. Sunstein (Chicago: University of Chicago Press, 1992), 189-190.

Introduction

The Name Game

Plato believed that ideas could be defined with absolute precision. He saw definitions of justice, goodness, beauty, et al., as embodied in universal forms that subsisted beyond the changes, variables, and vicissitudes of life around us. These forms could be represented by definitions which were true regardless of where one lived or from what perspective one spoke. They were absolute. They were so enraptured above the relativities of culture that even if the nature of justice might differ in Athens and Thrace, there still existed outside of this shadowy world, untouched by its diversity and change, a universal form of justice by which one could judge between the cultures and discern to what extent they conform to its true meaning. The goal of philosophy was to ascend to these heavenly ideals and establish definitions that would reveal the true nature of things here on earth.

This mission, however, did not prove to be so simple for Plato's heirs in the history of philosophy. The Sophists, who contended with Plato during his day over this matter, relegated all philosophical debates to a semantic exercise or cultural perspective; the Nominalists, in the Middle Ages, wondered whether universals were anything other than a collection of names that we use to refer to our own, arbitrary constructs. Philosophers today seem to have abandoned the project entirely as they consider words to slip and slide with usage, and definitions to be problematic, at best.

Richard Rorty, one of today's leading philosophers, is representative of this trend in linguistics. He finds it difficult not only to define specific terms but even to define the discipline to which he and Plato are supposed to belong. Philosophy, he says, has no specific form or matter or one thing in common. It might have a tradition by which it directs us to study a certain group of individuals throughout history, but what they all have in common is somewhat difficult to discern. Some study ethics, others reject its study. Some engage in metaphysical quests; others limit our knowledge to the world around us. Some try to analyze our minds; others prefer to study language and abandon the quest for knowledge altogether.

This same ambiguity in defining terms seems to plague the subject matter of religion in particular. The term "religion" is applied in our culture by all sorts of people in all sorts of ways to label an individual or group with whom they agree, disagree, or simply wish to study. Buddhism, for example, is often studied by religion departments in world religion courses at universities in this country, and is labeled as a religion in common usage. Yet, Buddha himself seems to be most agnostic toward matters that are often associated with the term religion. He did not speculate over the typical metaphysical issues that mark many religious discussions. He did not speculate over the existence of God or an afterlife. In fact, much like an atheist, he felt that such speculations would only detract from our focus upon the here and now, and if anything, he would prefer us to cultivate our own, individual responsibility instead of waiting for help outside ourselves, from the heavens above or the world to come. In order to attain Nirvana (i.e., in its original sense, a "cooling down" of life's passions), it is necessary to gain control of our lives and make a concerted effort to follow the techniques that he prescribes in the eightfold path. In this way Buddha offered his people nothing more than a way of coping with the throes and vicissitudes of this life, and believed that matters of metaphysical concern would detract from this overall mission.

Buddha's antipathy toward other religious forms also tends to dominate the Christian faith, especially among its conservative wing. These Christians emphasize the unique nature of the revelation of God in Christ and the qualitative distinction between those who practice other religious forms and what they believe and practice. Even though culture wishes to label the Christian faith as a religion, the conservatives often spurn this label and prefer not to be identified with the many groups defined as religions, as if possessing what is common to the many was bad. Karl Barth, the most celebrated theologian in the twentieth century, reveals this conservative aversion when he asserts that "the piety of man is vain blasphemy and the greatest of all the sins that he commits." He believes that it is against the very first of God's commandments to speculate about the divine nature and build idolatrous forms of human construction (Exod. 20:4, Rom. 1:21-23). In religion, this is exactly what is done. Here the human race talks without listening. It ventures to find God through its own intellectual and spiritual powers but does not heed what God has provided in His revelation. It believes in its own ability and activity but does not trust in the revelation and grace that God freely offers in Christ. For Barth and the conservatives, there can be no compromise on this point. Religion is the true negation of revelation and needs to be confessed, not coddled. There can be no coordination between the revelation of God and the quest of religion to find God through its own piety.[1]

Political reasons sometimes motivate certain groups in their use of the term "religion." These groups can use the term in describing themselves, if they feel that it will provide them with a special advantage or special favor from society. The "church" of Scientology is a good example of this type of political manipulation, as it fought the IRS long and hard in order to be classified as a religious, and therefore tax-exempt, group. The IRS had difficulty discerning the relationship that the group claimed to have with normative religious expression. Scientology offers personal happiness and success to those who practice its counseling methods and follow the writings of its founder, L. Ron Hubbard, a science fiction writer—all of which might be interesting and edifying; but is it religion?

The same game is played by a number of left-wing political groups in an attempt to elevate their own agenda to the exclusion of others. This time the name game is played by labeling their opponents' views as religious and decrying the destructive nature that religion presents to society as a whole. The most notorious of these groups is the Communist Party, which denounces religion in general and supports atheism. Karl Marx, in a scintillating criticism of the religion of his day, complained that the ideas of religion are shaped by the ruling class and its needs. "Religion is the opiate of the people," according to Marx. It injects into the soul of the working class, passive qualities like kindness, meekness, and gentleness, and tells them to submit to their master's whip without complaint. It tells them, "Don't worry or be overly concerned about your station in the here and now. All will be rectified in the end, when we meet Jesus." In response to such teaching, Karl Marx resolved to curse all religion as evil and demanded complete social revolution, including the expulsion of religion from society. He proclaimed himself to be an atheist and proceeded to reduce life to a dialectical and material struggle among economic forces. Life is a struggle for power between the rich and the poor. His exhortation to the working class was to arise and abolish all present institutions and ideologies as a product of bourgeois culture.

However, Marx's renunciation of religion only belies his own ideological commitments. Even if his criticisms are valid, religious principles are continuously invoked through-

out his work in order to promote his cause and the validity
of his analysis. In fact, they appear much more clearly in his
work than in the bourgeois, capitalistic doctrines, which he
denounced as such. As a follower of Georg Hegel, a most
God-intoxicated philosopher, Marx does not see history in
a Darwinian manner of endless change but in a teleological
manner much like a theist, marching toward an absolute,
ultimate goal. More than this, his zeal burns not for a material
goal, as one might expect, but a metaphysical ideal—a supreme, all-encompassing belief in social justice and equality.
This valuation of life in ethical and ideal terms, Marx did
not derive from a scientific analysis of this world. It is here
that he burns with the same righteous indignation of any
prophet, yearning for the will of God to descend upon a lost
and fallen world. With his followers, this vision was subject
to religious devotion. Marx became a cult-like figure, and
his vision a unifying, totalitarian system, by which all of life
must be subsumed and encompassed by certain values.

> [T]he Communist ideology constitutes a mythic
> framework for life, providing both a motivation for
> idealism and a validation of the existing social order;
> and the Communist Party is, sociologically, a church
> with its own hierarchy, its sacred scriptures, its sys-
> tem of dogma, including doctrines of the fall (the
> development of capitalism) and eschatology (the even-
> tual classless society), and having its exegetical dis-
> putes and heresies.[2]

In the United States, left-wing political groups such as
the American Civil Liberties Union (ACLU), People for
the American Way, and Americans United for Separation
of Church and State, play the same game. They inculcate
values in a most absolute and legalistic manner but deny any
connection between their ideas and religion. It is their opponents' ideas that must be labeled as religious and kept at
all costs from the public forum. This time, instead of elimi-
nating religion *in toto*, as the communists, they prefer to
make it a private matter, erect a wall of separation between

church and state, and prevent the state from indirectly or
directly "advancing religion." The government is called to
be neutral in matters of religious concern, even if it can and
must advance its own system of values. Here is some of the
rhetoric:

> Similarly, government must be scrupulous, no matter
> how much pressure it feels, to remain neutral in re-
> gard to all religious matters. . . . The Establishment
> clause ought to mean that neither directly nor indi-
> rectly should government be in the business of sup-
> porting religious activities. We have to understand
> that they (religious conservatives) have a right to hold
> those beliefs, but we have a right to demand that in
> the secular setting the metaphysical is not what ulti-
> mately should decide laws . . . children are taught the
> difference between right and wrong in the classroom
> every day. . . . For example, virtually every public
> school corridor, from elementary school to high
> school, has a poster communicating the message,
> "Don't Use Drugs!" I will let you in on a very poorly
> kept secret. Public schools are already teaching
> values. . . . Public schools are saturated with
> values. . . . The Public schools should focus on core
> values. It is unnecessary to label them with a reli-
> gious designation. These values are universal and stand
> just fine on their own.[3]

The outrageous nature of these comments needs to be
challenged, and it is the purpose of this book to provide that
challenge. If it were not for the steady drumming of secular
forces in our society, that espouse the wall of separation, it
might not be necessary to say much at all. But let's face it,
in the land of Thomas Jefferson, Hugo Black, and Madalyn
Murray O'Hair, many Americans can no longer hear the
serious flaws in this line of reasoning, however apparent.
Social conditioning promotes it, and Americans tend to
believe it, no matter how absurd it might be. After all, what
could be more absurd to anyone who knows a little about

the history of this country than the notion that doctrines so fundamental to our public life, doctrines that were conceived in this country through Christian and Puritan labor, doctrines such as liberty, equality, and democracy, could somehow be divorced from their religious roots and become at this present time secular by-products? Can ideas lose their original justification after a certain period of time and become the domain of a secular world, as if spiritual amnesia sets in? And even if one could forget the past, how could one justify these values or whatever values the State might preach without resorting to religious or metaphysical categories? Do admonitions like "don't use drugs" exist outside religious concern? Certainly, most philosophers would find such an enterprise to be facetious at best. It is religion, after all, that is most intimately involved with constructing systems of value. Whatever ethical system or beliefs one might wish to espouse—capitalism or communism, democracy or aristocracy, equality or inequality—it is difficult to see how one could derive it from a simple, secular description of the world as it is. Ethical admonitions speak of what *ought* to occur in this world, and assume some ideal or absolute vantage point in doing so. This makes the very notion of secular ethics fraught with difficulties as it contains no ideal perspective or divine standard to provide a foundation for its suppositions. Many philosophers would consider it a vacuous notion, if not an outright contradiction in terms. It certainly is difficult to understand how one could separate ethical concerns from the sphere of metaphysics, and so divide the mission of the state from a religious view of life.

Regardless of how one feels about this matter, it is difficult to deny that the triumph of church/state separation in the twentieth century has created a culture in which the secular reigns supreme and the sacral is relegated to an inferior position in society. When one drops an iron curtain somebody is being left out. The iron curtain between the church and the state has relegated religious people and their faith to a secondary role in a secular society and often pro-

vides those who come under the rubric of secularity with a
public platform by which to promote their own antireligious
agenda. The signs of the times are all around us. Textbooks
depict the rule of the church in the Middle Ages as a "dark
age" and the revival of paganism/humanism in the fourteenth century as the "rebirth" of humanity. Movies focus
upon the witch hunts and scarlet letters of Puritan New
England, portraying religion through those events as fanatical and bigoted. Television links "fundamentalism" with
terrorist activity in the Middle East, as if conservative religion is responsible and Muslims in general are not conservative.

These and other signs are used by some to show that
the secular world is downright hostile when it comes to its
portrayal and treatment of religion, especially certain forms
of religion like fundamentalism, which it does not like.
Michael Medved's *Hollywood v. America* is an excellent example of this type of literature.[4] Of course, one could deny
all this and point to a number of examples where the media,
Hollywood, and the powers-that-be have treated the religious community in a more positive light. It would certainly
be a daunting task to refute such a personal judgment. How
could one add up all the positive and negative comments
and arrive at a final score? What vantage point would one
use in assessing the comments? A neutral one? Perhaps it
would be better in the end to dispense with all matters of
judgment, leaving this business to God, and exhort all of us
to become more sensitive and fair in our dealings with one
another.

Beyond this simple exhortation, we must confess that
our primary concern lies elsewhere. Our primary concern is
not to attack antireligious bias, but to show that religious
assumptions are inherent in whatever we do in the private
or public sphere. It matters not what one's outward disposition toward religion might be, whether one is for it or
against it, whether one believes this or that. All of it displays
religious concern. All of it involves religious suppositions.
None of it can escape the presence of God.

It is here that we find the reason for writing this book—to bring glory to the God who is over all and under all and in all. This is the reason, the only *raison d'être* for which our society, its church, and the writing of a book could exist. Whether wittingly or unwittingly, all must bring glory to God—the brothers of Joseph through their jealousy (Gen. 50:20), Pharaoh through his hardened heart (Rom. 9:17), and Caiaphas through the sacrifice of Jesus for the people (John 11:50). No matter how depraved these people and their deeds might be, one cannot escape the presence of God or defy his counsels. He "works all things according to the counsel of His will" (Eph. 1:11). All must bring glory to God. "For from Him and through Him and unto Him are all things. To Him be the glory forever! Amen" (Rom. 11:36).

Notes

1. *Church Dogmatics*, ed. G. W. Bromiley and T. F. Torrance (Edinburgh: T. & T. Clark, 1963), I/1, 292ff.

2. J. Hick, *An Interpretation of Religion* (New Haven: Yale University Press, 1989), 22.

3. "Church and State" 44:152 (July-August 1991); 45: 261 (D 1992); 47:143 (June 1994); 48: 5 (January 1995); 48: 246 (D 1995).

4. Medved cites a *Public Opinion* survey of the most influential leaders within TV's creative community. Of the 104 surveyed, 45 percent claimed no religious affiliation and 93 percent never or seldom attended religious services. *Hollywood vs. America: Popular Culture and the War on Traditional Values* (Grand Rapids: Zondervan, 1992), 70-71.

CHAPTER I

The Puritan Heritage

The spiritual heritage of American culture cannot be denied by those who possess a most rudimentary knowledge of its past. Throughout much of its history, America has proclaimed itself to be a Christian nation with a manifest destiny before God. Many of its early settlers came to inhabit this land for the specific purpose of building a community that would honor their religious commitments. Most of the framers of its Constitution were members of Orthodox Christian denominations and employed those beliefs in establishing its laws. Many of its great presidents—George Washington, Abraham Lincoln, Teddy Roosevelt, Woodrow Wilson, etc.—linked their political causes with God and the injunctions of Scripture. It was a matter of public policy to seek divine guidance in all things and ask for divine blessing on the nation in its endeavors.[1] Abraham Lincoln declared, in calling a national day of prayer:

> [I]t is the duty of nations as well as of men, to own
> their dependence upon the overruling power of God,
> to confess their sins and transgressions, in humble
> sorrow, yet with assured hope that genuine repen-
> tance will lead to mercy and pardon; and to recog-

nize the sublime truth, announced in the Holy Scrip-
tures and proven by all history, that those nations
only are blessed whose God is the Lord.[2]

This profession of faith cannot be interpreted as mere
window dressing on policies that were inspired by other
motives. It speaks most emphatically from the religious matrix
out of which the nation's policies were forged at one time.
In fact, this religious matrix cannot be separated from the
basic laws, general ethos, and political policies that our founding fathers bequeathed to the culture as a whole. According
to most sociologists and historians, the culture bears the
indelible and unmistakable mark of its religious origin within
many of its most fundamental beliefs. While Americans no
longer associate democracy, capitalism, pragmatism, and empirical science with religious concerns, these articles of faith
are considered, within academic circles, to contain the imprint of their Puritan origin in a most decided way. They
remain filled with the religious inspiration of the past and
bear the same sort of implications in the present. Even if
other forces might have contributed to their expression in
the past and are evident in their statement today, it is not
possible to divide the sacral and the secular content of these
matters in the simple manner that the proponents of church/
state separation would wish to divide the culture and its
beliefs. It would be like dividing the Puritan community
into separate elements, when all things existed together in
its world as one people before God (*corpus Christianum*). It
would involve making simplistic distinctions and arbitrary
definitions—all for the sake of separating what is indistin-
guishable in that culture as well as our own.

The basic outline of American government was forged
during the seventeenth century by the English philosopher,
John Locke, a man of decided Puritan sympathies. He was
reared in a home of that persuasion, where his father was a
captain in a voluntary regiment of the parliamentary army.
He came under its influence once again when he matricu-
lated into Oxford during the period of the great Puritan

revolution and Cromwell's tenure as its chancellor. He later became a political refugee for his advocacy of their cause against the crown and the Anglican majority, and lived in Holland among other dissidents—Arminians, Anabaptists (Mennonites), Separatists, et al.—who helped to strengthen his call for political freedom and religious tolerance.

It was after this time that John Locke wrote his most influential and well-received treatise on political philosophy, *Concerning Civil Government, Second Essay* (1690). This treatise contains the fundamental features and basic outline of the American form of government. It also contains the unmistakable imprint of his background as a religious dissident and cannot be separated from it.[3]

The government, which he erected in this work, is clearly built upon religious principles. In contrast to other political philosophers of the era (e.g., Hobbes, Rousseau, and Hume), Locke refused to make public policy subservient to the capricious nature of social norms. He believed that there is a universal law, implanted in nature by God and known by all human beings, regardless of their position in life. This law serves as the supreme rule of all people, and the preservation of its truth must be the fundamental concern of government.

> It is a power that hath no other end but preservation, and therefore can never have a right to destroy, enslave, or designedly to impoverish the subjects; the obligations of the law of Nature cease not in society, but only in many cases are drawn closer, and have, by human laws, known penalties annexed to them to enforce their observation. Thus the law of Nature stands as an eternal rule to all men, legislators as well as others. The rules that they make for other men's actions must, as well as their own and other men's actions, be conformable to the law of Nature—*i.e.*, to the will of God, of which that is a declaration, and the fundamental law of Nature being the preservation of mankind, no human sanction can be good or valid against it.[4]

This law can be derived from a number of sources in the history of western culture. It finds expression in a number of Graeco-Roman philosophers—Aristotle, Epictetus, Seneca, Cicero, and many others. It is espoused by Christian theologians throughout its history—its most eloquent spokesmen being the Apostle Paul in the early church, Thomas Aquinas in the Middle Ages, and Philipp Melanchthon in the Reformation. It is espoused by all factions of the Reformation and would have been an integral part of Locke's religious training. Locke cites Richard Hooker's *Laws of Ecclesiastical Polity* (I.10) at several junctures to substantiate his concept, but the specific source does not really matter. The doctrine of the natural law is a typical part of the western religious tradition and cannot be understood apart from this heritage. The concept is innately religious as it looks to that which is universal, absolute, and transcendent to exact its demands. It believes that there is a will of God, which transcends all social norms and serves as the metaphysical ideal for all of humanity to follow.

According to Locke, the government derives its fundamental purpose in preserving the rights that are given to all in nature. A legislative branch of government is needed to spell out these rights in written form, so that no one can neglect them or feign ignorance. According to Puritan tradition, the natural law needs a more precise, written form in order to clear up the bleary-eyed vision that we have of God and his law in nature. The legislature and the other branches of government are needed to supply what is lacking in nature due to our own insufficiencies. This relates not only to our need for written laws but also to our need for a civil power to interpret, judge, and execute the laws. It is dangerous to give these matters over to human bias and allow the natural man to exact vengeance on his own accord. Along with a legislative branch, federative and executive branches of government are needed, because nature lacks a judge to determine differences and an executioner to protect the citizenry against domestic and foreign enemies. The three branches of government are needed to preserve the natural rights of the citizenry and insure that the natural law is fulfilled in an orderly and just manner. These three branches of government characterize much of Locke's political philosophy and will become most associated with the American system, which is governed by a legislative, executive, and judicial branch.[5]

The content of the natural law and the rights that it affords to all is listed in varying forms throughout the treatise. They typically and succinctly include the following trilogy: life, liberty, and possessions. The term "life" refers to the right of the people to protect their lives and resist the arbitrary acts of criminals and tyrants against oneself or others; "liberty" is the right to be free from coercive power, which would enslave someone to another's will; and "possessions" is the right to own the property over which one labors and toils.[6]

Along with life, liberty, and possessions, Locke also emphasizes the belief that everyone is created equal. By this he means that no one is born with blue blood flowing in his or her veins, as if possessing a natural right to rule over others by the mere fact of one's birth. One could just as easily be born in a log cabin and possess "the right stuff" to rule over a great nation. Equality, along with liberty and property rights, will become the most emblematic members of his analysis of the natural law.[7] They will become the shibboleths of modern, western culture, and they will become embodied in the American psyche as "inalienable rights." Its people will come to demand a "Bill of Rights" in order to protect these and other rights from the incursions of federal government.

Liberty

Liberty is the most important of the inalienable rights which Locke puts forth in his analysis. It is "the foundation of all the rest," because a government that would deign to take away this right can proceed to dispose of all the rest. It works itself out in a number of different forms within his treatise, but none serve his purposes or those of the American people more than the emphasis that he places upon religious toleration and democratic rule. These two aspects of liberty become the basic pillars of his concept, as well as that of the western world, and deserve a more detailed look.

Locke was an advocate of religious toleration throughout his career. He believed that the purpose of government is to protect the basic rights of its citizens, not to bring salvation to their souls or coerce them into a specific or detailed form of belief. Government should not be concerned with the profession or conduct of a people, as long as they do not cause injury one to another. Government should only punish those matters that "are prejudicial to other men's rights" or represent a threat to "the public peace of societies."[8]

The church itself has no interest in coercing others to comply. True Christianity does not convert by the sword. Toleration is "the chief characteristic mark" of its fellowship. It knows that delivering a heretic to be burned at the stake does not deliver that soul from the flames of a burning hell. Coercion cannot produce heartfelt repentance or faith in those who suffer under the methods of papal inquisitions. It is not faith but the avarice of ambitious leaders which forwards these persecutions. Their motives have little to do with truth but the expansion of their own ecclesiastical dominion. The true church is a voluntary or free society, which derives its laws from the common consent of that society, and not from the incursion of political or ecclesiastical authorities.[9]

In this context, Locke follows the example of many of the dissident groups of the day, who preferred to accent the New Testament over the Old Testament as a more perfect paradigm of godly living. Locke says that the people of old were given a law at Mount Sinai, which pertained to them alone and not to the rest of the human race.[10] They were given the sword as a nation to establish God's rule—Joshua,

David, Josiah, et al. But the New Testament did not continue this establishment or constitute a theocratic kingdom
of its own, in which every idolatry and transgression would
receive a just and swift recompense. Jesus and his disciples
suffered at the hands of those who wielded the sword. They
established their church on a message of love and forgiveness, yielding all judgment upon evil to the wrath of God
and the dawning of His kingdom in the latter days. The
sword was not used as a part of their arsenal or program. It
could not effectively vanquish their foe—a foe that lurked in
dark places and spiritual realms—a foe that could withstand
all the weaponry of human invention—a foe that could only
be vanquished by the power of the divine Word.

Jesus did not offer himself as a political Messiah to
those who preferred a worldly kingdom of power and privilege. He did not fight the power brokers of the day with the
weapons of this world, who spat at Him, flogged Him, and
put Him to death. He did not send twelve legions of angels
to withstand the temple guard that came to arrest Him
(Matt. 26:53). He did not reply in like manner to those who
accused Him of falsehood and blasphemy (Matt. 27:12-14).
He did not dispatch an army of His followers to fight the
Romans and their designs to have Him crucified. He told
Pilate that His "kingdom was not of this world," otherwise
He and His disciples would fight (John 18:36). He told His
disciples to reject the rulers of this world, who "lord it over
those allotted to their charge," and follow His example of
humility and servanthood. He told them that if they wanted
to follow Him, they must take up their cross and do as He
did. "For even the Son of Man came not to be served but
to serve, and give His life as a ransom for many" (Mark
8:34; 10:42-45).

The church was faithful to this commission in much of
its early history. Most of the original disciples and many in
the early church did not resist those who persecuted them
but were led away as martyrs to experience a most agonizing
death. Christians refused to participate in the political and

military might of the Roman Empire, rejecting its brutality and cultic forms. Even when the empire was being sacked by barbarous hordes, Christians refused to defend its interests as well as their own property through the use of the sword, incurring the disdain of other citizens.[11]

However, this all changed when Constantine, the Roman emperor, became a "Christian" in the fourth century. He believed that the god of Christianity had brought him victory in battle over his enemies through a vision, which he beheld of the cross, and so Christianity began to sanction the use of the sword thereafter as a means of defending its Holy Roman Empire. With Theodosius I, Christianity became the official religion of the State in (380). It made the transition from being the persecuted to becoming the persecutor during this period, even though its coercive power will not become appreciable for some time. Theodosius attempted to insure the unanimity of his subjects under one orthodox confession—the Niceno-Constantinopolitan Creed, which speaks of the divine nature of the Father, Son, and Holy Spirit. In the Middle Ages, spiritual courts went on to burn heretics at the stake, and crusaders slaughtered religious infidels in order to rid the Holy Land of their presence.

The church's exercise of temporal power became embodied during this time in one office and one man. In the early church, there was a plurality of bishops or elders who ruled over the affairs of the church. This situation began to change in the first part of the second century, when the so-called monarchical bishops arose and ruled as one man over the church in each city. Ignatius, the first of these bishops, forbad the church of Antioch to meet or celebrate its rituals without him and placed himself at the top of the church's hierarchy as ruling "in the place of God." Eventually the bishops of the major cities vied for prestige and power throughout the Roman empire. It is the bishop of Rome who will win this battle and become the head of the Catholic or universal church. Leo will call himself the "bishop of bishops," as the true successor of Peter, the greatest of the Apostles in authority. He claims that Christ had bestowed special authority on Peter during his earthly ministry (Matt. 16:18-19), and the successors of Peter's bishopric in Rome—a matter of historical dispute—are afforded the same, special authority. Leo will gain a strategic victory at the council of Chalcedon (451) when he puts forth a solution to the Christological problems of the day, and he will gain ascendancy over other major sees, who were tainted by the conflict.

The power of the Pope grew throughout most of the Middle Ages to encompass many areas of civil concern. This worldly power served as a means of corrupting both the institution and the church through its wealth, land, and armies. Popes will exercise authority over the rulers of nations and make them cower before their priestly powers. Pope Gregory VII (1073-1085) excommunicated Henry IV, suspended him from exercising royal powers, and released his subjects in Germany and Italy from their oath of allegiance when the latter tried to intrude on his powers. In one of the most telling scenes in church history, Henry IV is seen in penitential garb, in the dead of winter, in bare feet, pleading to be reinstated into the Pope's favor, because his subjects were about to depose him from office in accordance with papal demands. Other Popes acted in like manner throughout the Middle Ages. When Henry II sought to defy the Pope and put the Archbishop of Canterbury, Thomas Becket, to death for criticizing the defiance, Pope Alexander III (1159-1181) proceeded to canonize Becket, which resulted in streams of pilgrims kneeling before the saint's tomb; he also had the king flogged before the tomb as an act of penance. The Popes could make and unmake kings in accordance with their good pleasure. The zenith of this power might have been reached by Innocent III (1198-1216), when he declared himself to be the "Vicar of Christ" and "the judge of all men and judged by none." But the most corrupt of them all had to be Pope Alexander VI

(1492-1503), whom Machiavelli depicts as the personifica-
tion of pure hypocrisy. This Pope bribed his way into office,
lived an opulent life-style, placed his own children over several
sees, aggrandized his relatives, seized property, executed dissidents, conducted assassinations, and eventually died from
a poison that he had concocted for one of his rivals.

It was in this context that cries for the separation of
church and state began to emerge in the modern world.
These cries were not directed against the government's entanglement with religion, as if society would be better off
without divine guidance and its leadership less corrupt. The
particular concern was for the purity of the church and the
corrupting nature that the temporal powers had brought
upon the papacy and its institutions. The main goal was to
cleanse the church from that which continues to corrupt the
political world—the money, the power, the pomp—so that it
could serve once again as a light in the world and not be
shrouded in the darkness of its lusts.

These cries can be heard within the church in the late
Middle Ages, but all of the discontent came to a head during the Protestant Reformation of the sixteenth century,
when church and society fractured over the issue. Martin
Luther, a monk and professor from Germany, spearheaded
the movement. He denounced the church for selling par-
dons (indulgences) for money in order to fund building
projects. He denounced its use of the sword to implement
religious dogma and punish reformers. He thought that the
church should rid itself of the use of temporal powers all
together. There are two kingdoms in this world which need
to remain distinct: the temporal kingdom, which compels
its citizens into an outward civility or righteousness (*iustitia
civilis*), and the spiritual kingdom, which forgives the most
vile of sinners for their crimes against God freely and without punishment. Both kingdoms have their anointing before God, and both can provide a place of service for the
Christian. But they cannot be reconciled with each other.
The former contains an "alien work" of God, accomplishing

its role through the most suspect of means, while the latter contains the "proper work" of God as it dispenses divine mercy and forgiveness to those who heed its message. The church must remain within its own mission and fulfill the role that God has assigned to it in the present age.[12]

John Calvin, the Reformer from Geneva, followed Luther's lead and spoke of the relationship between church and state in much the same way. In his *Institutes of the Christian Faith*, the most celebrated theology of the Reformation, Calvin condemned the worldly power of the pope and the church in the Middle Ages, its "battles, bloodshed, slaughter of armies, sacking of some cities, destruction of others, massacres of nations, and devastations of kingdoms— solely to seize other men's dominions." The church does not have the authority to punish, compel, or force. It does not have "the right of the sword." That right is reserved for the magistrate and the civil authorities. The spiritual kingdom must be kept "completely distinct" from the civil kingdom, so that the church will not become caught up in "worldly elements." This, of course, does not mean that the government is irreligious or has no anointing from God. Calvin believed that it must protect the cause of religion, defend the position of the church, encourage piety, prevent open sacrilege and public offenses against religion. It must promote religion in general, but it cannot use the power of the sword to establish a specific form of religion through coercive or legalistic means.[13]

Nevertheless, the mainline Reformers were not so consistent or radical in their adherence to these principles as the dissidents of the time wanted. It was the dissidents of the Reformation who fought most consistently to separate church and state, even to the point of spilling their own blood. The earliest and most influential of these groups was the Anabaptists, who had their origin in Switzerland and Southern Germany. They were persecuted unmercifully in the sixteenth century for their radical attempts at reform, especially in regard to the relationship of church and state, which they incessantly criticized. They went so far as to oppose all participation of Christians in government as "outside the perfection of Christ"—a position that did not endear them to the magistrates of Christian nations. (Even Luther, who considered rulers to be "the worst knaves" and "the greatest fools," did not presume to call them infidels.) The position of the Anabaptists was brash and dangerous at this time, but they claimed it was most consonant with the example of Christ and his followers as set forth in the New Testament. Christ and his disciples did not use the methods of this world to coerce others into conformity with their religious principles. They did not become involved in the political process of the day as kings or zealots but separated themselves from its evils and suffered at the hands of its godless leaders. The Anabaptists considered the example of the New Testament to be applicable in a most literal manner to their own day and age. It had priority over the Old Testament and its theocratic kingdom as a more perfect revelation of God's will for his servants in the present dispensation. Some of the Anabaptist leaders were even willing to advocate a pluralistic society in which Jews, Turks, pagans, and Christians could live together unmolested, despite the differences between them.[14]

John Locke came into direct contact with this position during his time as a political refugee in Holland. Holland was known as a haven for a number of dissident religious groups during the Reformation. The Anabaptists were represented in the low-countries by the Mennonites, who found the spiritual climate most auspicious for their beliefs. Among the groups of like-spirit, the Arminians were most prominent in withstanding the religious compulsion of the political and ecclesiastical establishment in the land. John Locke was certainly appreciative of their contribution for the cause of liberty. He befriended Phillip Limborch, one of their leaders, and had some limited correspondence with him concerning their mutual cause and plight.

The Arminians were particularly concerned with pro-

viding latitude for Christians to study the Scripture on their
own in doctrinal areas. Their belief that human beings possessed the freedom to accept or reject divine grace had caused
them to be persecuted by the Dutch Reformed Church;
which believed in the absolute sovereignty of God in matters of salvation. James Arminius believed that disputed areas
such as the question of divine sovereignty and human freedom should not be settled through a creed of the church or
a synod appointed by the magistrate. These are areas in
which the Scripture is not so clear, and each believer should
be free to develop his or her own interpretation. Simon
Episcopius, the student and close friend of Arminius, led
the appeal for toleration at the Synod of Dort, when opponents had convened to pass judgment upon Arminian doctrine. In an oration before the Synod, Episcopius proposed
that mutual tolerance should rule over the church in disputed areas and cited a number of instances where such
amiable policies prevailed in the Reformed Church during
that era, but all to no avail. Phillip Limborch later discredited the decrees of all ecclesiastical councils as subject to
corruption and error and unnecessary to the well-being of
the church. There might be some "Fundamental Articles of
the Faith," which all Christians should believe, but he considered these to be few and far between. Each of the faithful
can serve as "his own judge" in doctrinal matters and determine the genuine sense from the false without the aid of
synods, creeds, or inquisitions. No governmental authority
is absolutely necessary for the church to extirpate heresy.
One should never inflict corporal punishment in matters of
religious conscience.[15]

Many dissident groups carried the spirit of liberty a step
further and brought its message to bear upon the very structure of the churches they founded. They brought liberty into
the church in the form of more congregational participation
in its affairs, and some went so far as to advocate a democratic polity. This teaching was a natural development of the
Reformation's distaste for the papal hierarchy and Luther's

accent upon the priesthood of the believers. It was also
consonant with Christ's own rejection of the political and
religious authorities of His day, and His exhortation to the
disciples to act like brothers and servants to one another.

The group that proved to have the most direct influence
upon Locke, America, and the future of democracy was
their own Puritan forebears. Puritanism arose in England
after Henry VIII broke with the church of Rome in the
1530s and became a continued source of agitation in its
attempt to exorcise Roman practices from the Anglican
Church. Congregationalism developed among the radical
fringe of the Puritans in the 1580s when Robert Browne,
Robert Harrison, and others became frustrated with the
progress of the reform and formed their own, separatist
church. Browne believed that the true church was far removed from the universal, totalitarian visions of Rome. It
consisted of individual congregations who had their own,
separate covenants, elected their own ministers, and pre-
sided over their own affairs.

Congregational polity became an important feature of
the Puritan churches that were planted in New England
during the seventeenth century. The first Puritan Church in
this country, established in Salem (1629), was formed according to the congregational model. This church and others like it saw each congregation as a self-sufficient, autonomous league, bound by its own covenant, exercising its own
discipline, electing its own officials, and governing its own
affairs. John Cotton, the leading theologian of the day, said
that no mother church should have the "power of Government over another, but each of them hath chiefe power
within itselfe, and all of them equall power one with another." While there might be a need for some association
with others, there is no need to recognize the authority of
Rome or England in governing local affairs. It is not the
pope or the king who rules the visible, militant church, but
Jesus Christ. "The Church is a mysticall body, whereof Christ
is the Head, the Members be Saints, called out of the world,

and united together into one Congregation, by an holy Covenant." Each church is compacted together through the parishioners' own voluntary consent. They agree to meet together as one congregation and do not even need officers to forge the covenant or serve their fellowship. The "brotherhood" has the authority to elect their own officers and members, and they have the authority to dismiss or excommunicate them.[16]

> This *Form* is the *Visible Covenant*, Agreement or consent whereby they give up themselves unto the Lord, to the observing of the ordinances of Christ together in the same society, which is usually called the *Church-Covenant;* For wee see not otherwise how members can have *Church-power* one over another mutually.... This Voluntary *Agreement, Consent or Covenant* (for all these are here taken for the same): Although the more express & plain it is, the more fully it puts us in mind of our mutuall duty, & stirreth us up to it, & leaveth lesse room for the questioning of the Truth of the *Church-estate* of a Company of professors, & the Truth of membership of particular persons: [6] yet wee conceive, the substance of it is kept, where there is a real Agreement & consent, of a company of faithful persons to meet constantly together in one Congregation, for the publick worship of God, & their mutuall edification: which real agreement & consent they doe express by their constant practise in comming together for the publick worship of God, & by their religious subjection unto the ordinances of God there: the rather, if wee doe consider how Scripture covenants have been entred into, not only expressly by word of mouth, but by sacrifice; by hand writing, & seal; & also somtimes by silent consent, without any writing, or expression of words at all.... The power graunted by Christ unto the body of the church & *Brotherhood*, is a prerogative or priviledge which the church doth exercise: I In *Choosing* their own officers, whether El-

ders, or Deacons. II In *admission* of their own members & therefore, there is great reason they should
have power to *Remove* any from their fellowship
again.[17]

The principles of Puritan polity ended up permeating
their community and much of the country as a whole. It is
clear that the basic inspiration for democracy in this country
arose from this community. It did not arise so much in the
eighteenth century from plantation owners or future presidents from Virginia. In the south, where the Anglican
Church supplied much of the spiritual and political inspiration, an aristocracy ruled the church, the society, and the
government for much of its history before the Revolutionary
War. It was not the southern aristocracy that supplied the
initial inspiration for democracy in America but the Puritan
community in the north with its congregational polity and
town meetings. It was in this community that townships
became established in the mid-seventeenth century and the
people assembled together to vote over their own affairs. It
was the Puritan congregations and their townships that spread
the spirit of democracy throughout the country.

> Puritanism . . . corresponded in many points with the
> most absolute democratic and republican theories. It
> was this tendency that had aroused its most danger-
> ous adversaries. Persecuted by the government of the
> mother country, and disgusted by the habits of a
> society which the rigor of their own principles con-
> demned, the Puritans went forth to seek some rude
> and unfrequented part of the world where they could
> live according to their own opinions and worship
> God in freedom. . . . The general principles which
> are the groundwork of modern constitutions, prin-
> ciples which, in the seventeenth century, were im-
> perfectly known in Europe, and not completely tri-
> umphant even in Great Britain, were all recognized
> and established by the laws of New England: the
> intervention of the people in public affairs, the free

voting of taxes, the responsibility of the agents of power, personal liberty, and trial by jury were all positively established without discussion.[18]

Equality

In the seventeenth and eighteenth centuries, democracy was related to the concept of equality. Democracy meant, for its proponents, the equal participation of "all men" in the political process. John Locke disparaged the notion that certain families had a divine right to rule over others, as if they were superior by birth and natural endowment. Thomas Jefferson told King George that "all men are created equal," that the king is no better than anyone else, that all citizens share common rights which are meant to protect them against all forms of despotism. The cry for equality became a most distinguishing characteristic of the age, and its outworking still preoccupies the minds of its constituents in the modern world.

One could point to a number of historical roots for this doctrine, but none of them are more essential to its proliferation in our culture than its Christian background. The Christian faith arose during a cosmopolitan time, where cultures began to interact with one another through a universal language, a system of safe and efficient roads, and a peace imposed by the might of Rome. Philosophies were forged to reflect the universal spirit of the time. Stoics, for example, considered themselves to be world citizens and valued each and every individual in that world as necessary within the divine scheme of things. This philosophy and others helped to shape the spirit of the world in a number of areas and should be accorded a valued place in its tradition, but none of them will prove to be so essential as Christianity and its Gospel in purveying to the modern world the universal and egalitarian spirit of the time.

The egalitarian spirit of Christianity was first formulated in reaction to an aberrant form of Judaism, which grew up after the Babylonian captivity in the sixth century B.C.

The Jews were sent into captivity at that time as punishment for their many sins against the Lord. The prophets of the Old Testament considered the Jews to be personally responsible for their own fall from divine favor (Ezek. 18), but it was also clear to them that the influence of foreigners in the Holy Land and the surrounding regions had helped to corrupt their ways through idolatrous and immoral practices. The answer to the Jewish woes after the captivity came in the form of severe measures to restrict contact with corrupting influences. It came in the form of complete separation from alien elements, so that their presence might be removed as a source of temptation. For example, Ezra and Nehemiah, when they returned to the land following the captivity, demanded that the Jewish men who had married foreign women divorce them immediately and send them away, along with their children (Ezra 10, Neh. 10). This spirit of separation became an integral aspect of religious commitment. It came to typify the very religious leaders of the subsequent period as a sign of self-righteousness. The Pharisees or "separate ones" prided themselves in building a "fence" around the law and themselves, in order to reduce the possibility of temptation. They separated themselves not only from Gentiles but even from their own people, the so-called *am ha-aretz* (people of the land), who did not follow in a punctilious manner their traditional interpretations. It was beneath them to sit at a table with common people, who were not as knowledgeable or scrupulous in their practice of Levitical rituals and traditional rites of purity as they professed to be.

It was in this context that Christianity and its spirit of egalitarianism were born. Much of it was aimed against the Pharisees as a rebuke to their extreme measures and practices. Much of what Jesus did and said in His ministry was specifically designed to annoy their religious sensibilities. To aggravate the Pharisees, Jesus chose as His disciples uneducated, blue-collar workers from the region of Galilee, instead of Rabbis from Jerusalem. He defended His disciples when they failed to follow the purification ceremonies of punctilious, Pharisaic custom, and even flaunted His own liberty by breaking their strict observance of the Sabbath. He sat down at banquets to drink wine with tax-collectors and sinners. He conversed with Samaritans, Canaanites, and Romans, whom He declared to have greater faith than most Jews. He declared that God was now turning to the Gentiles to welcome them into His kingdom.

The Apostle Paul will carry this message of divine acceptance to the Gentiles during his missionary tours. Paul says that it is very much the heart of the Gospel—a truth without compromise—that the Gentiles, together with the Jews, are fellow-heirs, members, and partakers of the Gospel (Eph. 3:5, 6; Gal. 2). And this Gospel will include not only the integration of all races or nationalities but will be extended to other areas to include women, children, the poor, the oppressed, and even one's enemies. "There is neither Jew nor Greek, slave nor free, male nor female, for you are all one in Christ Jesus" (Gal. 3:28). [In Christ, God does not seem to recognize the artificial boundaries that humanity has erected against one another. He rejects any system of class through which the church would presume to honor the rich, the powerful, and the free (1 Cor. 1:26, James 2:1). If they are rich, they should only boast in their poverty; if they are poor, only in their riches (James 1:9, 10). He rejects all patriarchal societies in which men would desire fellowship with each other to the exclusion of women. Men without women are not men but alone and incomplete (1 Cor. 11:11, 12, Gen. 2:18). He even rejects those who would separate themselves from sinners as "smoke in My nostrils, a fire that keeps burning all day long" (Isa. 65:5). God has called His people not only to suffer at the hand of sinners but to confess their own solidarity with them as sinners. Christ told them not to judge but to love their enemies.]

The doctrine of equality has not always characterized the practice of the church throughout the ages, but it certainly has helped to change the surrounding culture into a more sublime image. In more recent times, Martin Luther King used the doctrine to fight the forces of segregation and racism in the American culture at large. He fought White supremacists, conservative apathy, southern segregationists, the Ku Klux Klan, and even the Black Muslims in his attempt to provide a semblance of decency and justice for his people. His political agenda was unashamedly a religious crusade, as he preached sermons, filled with religious rhetoric, on the most basic of Christian themes, i.e., egalitarianism and integration. Even his political tactics of passive resistance and love for one's enemies were drawn from the Sermon on the Mount and proved effective in shaming an angry public into national repentance.[19]

The doctrine of equality has also helped to stimulate the modern women's movement, although the religious implications are seldom acknowledged by its constituency. Feminists do not identify themselves with religion in any specific way and are sometimes hostile toward its more conservative forms, but their emphasis upon equality does betray at least some interest in the subject, and it cannot be otherwise. Even if one discounts the Christian origin of equality in the culture, the very invocation of the concept cannot be separated from religious concern, because it represents a metaphysical valuation. The belief in equality arises outside of empirical concerns and its simple, physical descriptions of this world. No empirical analysis of science can establish the value or worth of the objects it studies. No one can see with the naked eye notions of equality, fairness, decency, or worth. These notions are metaphysical and can only be seen through the eyes of faith. One who wishes to discount them and point to the empirical differences between men and women, can do so without contradiction or dispute from the laws of scientific observation. The doctrine of equality belongs to the laws of nature, which transcend those of scientific observation and judge us all.

Property

Religion and its principles are less explicit these days due to the secular forces that have attempted to discount their power. Left-wing, secular forces like to reduce life to material or economic concerns. Karl Marx liked to reduce the forces of life to a clash between competing social concerns, and thus the name "dialectical materialism" was used to describe his philosophy. Moral concerns, religious convictions, and the world of ideas are believed to be the product of one's economic status in life rather than the impetus through which social change is engendered. All things are said to arise from materialistic concerns. All things are subject to economic forces. Marx believed that the communist revolution would rupture the traditional ideas of the ruling class—ideas concerning religion, property, etc.—when the working class came to power and created their own ideas in accordance with their own material interests.[20]

Alexis de Tocqueville, who wrote the most definitive work on democracy in America, believed much the opposite. He thought that spirit was more important to the success of a people than their outward position in life. He felt that the customs of the American people were more important to their future than the physical circumstances of their birth or the legal structure of their government. It was the habits and opinions of a people that were most essential to what they did and achieved.

> There is hardly any human action, however particular it may be, that does not originate in some very general idea men have conceived of the Deity, of His relation to mankind, of the nature of their own souls, and of their duties to their fellow creatures. Nor can anything prevent these ideas from being the common spring from which all the rest emanates.[21]

The Puritans certainly did not come to this country on materialistic impulses seeking gold or silver but were particularly driven by an idea. They wanted to be free from papal and royal (Anglican) authority and establish their own form of Christianity in a new world. It was this religious impulse that led them to establish a society marked by a free political process and a free market economy. Democracy and capitalism conjoined in a community that first respected the autonomy and spirituality of its own individual members in its churches and religious ideals.[22]

Max Weber, the most renowned sociologist of this past century, tended to agree with Tocqueville's assessment of the issue more than he did with Marx's. He did not discount the importance of social conditions and environmental factors in shaping a culture, but he did feel that the spirit of a people was most essential to the process. Weber had no ax to grind. He was not a religious man, but he did appreciate the enormous impact that spiritual forces played in shaping the political and economic conditions around us. His particular case in point was the relationship between Calvinism and capitalism. He believed that the theology of the Reformation, as it was interpreted and advanced by the Calvinists (especially Puritans), provided the groundwork for the formation and expansion of capitalism. While other factors from the business world (e.g., bookkeeping) were important to its evolution, it was Calvinism that provided the most fertile ground for the new economic philosophy to prosper. It was in those towns, cities, and states associated with the spirit of Calvinism that capitalism began to flourish.[23]

According to Weber and Tocqueville, capitalism displays a certain spirit or vision in life, and this spirit became embodied within Puritanism. The Puritans reflect the spirit of a present day capitalist or entrepreneur—one who is adventuresome, one who is willing to surrender present security for future betterment, one who encourages risk, experiment, innovation, and development. They braved tempestuous seas during the seventeenth century to settle in a frontier filled with danger and uncertainty. They believed that change was good, the future was good, that they were a part of a historical process in which the kingdom of God would dawn. They hoped to build a society which would reflect that kingdom and prepare the world for its coming. Their spirit did not resign their people to the worship of tradition. Life was not a sacred circle of endless repetition. It was not a recurrence of ancestral ways or a closed-shell of unalterable laws, destined to repeat the status quo. Their paradigm was history, and in history life must move on. God and his people were working together in history to create a better world and prepare the way for His millennial kingdom—the goal to which all of history was moving.[24]

Therefore, the focus of the Puritan community was directed toward investing in their society and building a brighter tomorrow. These themes of Puritanism and capitalism can be found in a number of their divines, but none of them served the purposes of Weber's analysis more than Richard Baxter and his famous tome on Puritan ethics, *A Christian Directory* (1673). In this work, Baxter followed the analysis of the Reformers and other Puritan divines in condemning the monastic or contemplative life of medieval tradition as useless to the community. He believed that such a life had no utilitarian or practical use within the community as it benefited no one except oneself. "The first and principle thing" in life was to employ one's energy in "the service of God, and the publick good." And this applied not only to an idle or ascetic life but also to a hedonistic one, which would squander riches upon an extravagant life-style. Baxter did not so much condemn riches in their own right, but only if they were squandered on oneself and not invested within the community to enhance its wealth. One was commissioned to use riches or capital for the good of the community, not to consume them as a prodigal son upon the fine things of life.[25]

In this, Weber and other sociologists find the seeds of capitalism. Certainly, capitalists have shared throughout their history a similar philosophy of life. Adam Smith, the great apostle of capitalism, spoke in a similar vein when he condemned those who consumed wealth on extravagance or idleness. He believed, like the Puritans, that money or capital can become productive only if it is used to fund workers or buy machines.

> The proportion between capital and revenue, therefore, seems everywhere to regulate the proportion between industry and idleness. Wherever capital predominates, industry prevails: wherever revenue, idleness. Every increase or diminution of capital, therefore, naturally tends to increase or diminish the real quantity of industry, the number of productive hands, and consequently the exchangeable value of the annual produce of the land and labour of the country, the real wealth and revenue of all its inhabitants.[26]

Capitalists treat the making of money as a calling, but this is not so much to satisfy their greed or desire for things. Money is only valuable as a means of investing in the future, and it loses its generative power when consumed. Capitalists like John D. Rockefeller often live austere life-styles so that they will have more money to invest in their next enterprise. They choose to forgo present consumption, in order to reap a larger profit in the future. What makes them capitalists is not greed but the desire to utilize money, turn a profit, go out, and make more money.

The Puritans helped to facilitate the growth of capitalism by commending what capitalists must do in order to succeed. They must practice temperance or moderation in all things. According to William Perkins, riches should only be consumed to meet the needs of oneself or one's family. Otherwise they should be given to the poor, the church, or used for the "maintenance of the commonwealth." According to Baxter, the rich are beholden to mortify their flesh just as the poor. They should not overindulge in fine wines, exquisite foods, unproductive idleness, or "time-wasting" recreations. They are no more at liberty to indulge their lusts than the next person. Ostentation, pomp, luxury, and superfluities are strictly forbidden. "Excess" for Baxter is defined as spending money on unnecessary things, which could have been used for a greater good.[27]

If wasting money was a sin among Puritans, wasting time in idleness or frivolous behavior was the deadliest of all. Luther and the Reformation had rejected the contemplative life of the Middle Ages as speculative, idle, and unproductive. The religious life was to be lived no longer within the cloistered environment of a monastery in idle meditation but within the world and in active participation. The Puritans became the Reformation's most virulent critics of the contemplative life as it subverts what they considered to be the true calling of a Christian (i.e., to labor actively for the kingdom). "It is (by) action that God is most served and honored." They considered the span of life too short and too precious to be wasted in useless tasks, idle talk, or needless recreations; these matters are unprofitable and unproductive to the service of a community. All must labor for the benefit of humanity, and there are no exceptions. This applies to the rich and the poor alike, since God is no respecter of persons. There is no time for anyone to waste on personal pluming.[28]

In fact, labor becomes essential to one's relationship to God. One's standing before God depends upon the faithful fulfillment of one's calling in the world. There is no cheap grace or sacramental absolution for those who escape their duty. While salvation might not depend on works, it does result in a new life, lived in devotion and service to others. Good works are performed not to obtain or maintain one's relationship with God but to help the community and build a better world. This is the true sign of election. This is the proof that one's faith is genuine or the sign that God has truly brought his elective purposes to bear in your heart. It is not faith or simple trust in divine promises that brings assurance but the inspection of its fruit, the faithful and active participation of God's people in the world.[29]

This worldly asceticism is given a divine calling by the Puritans. What was considered secular work in former days is now considered a sacred calling before God. In the Middle Ages, those who chose a business career were considered lax in their moral thinking, or at least beneath those who served the church in a more direct way. But the Reformation changed all this. Luther elevated the status of the laity, declaring them to be priests before God, and consecrated their work in the world as a diving calling (*Beruf*). The Puritans made this doctrine of Luther's a centerpiece of their theology and teaching. They believed that the poorest cobbler has a more noble calling in life than the most pious, mendicant monk. They asserted that every person has been set apart by God with a special calling, not just the clergy— whether one serves as a magistrate, physician, lawyer, or school teacher. The important matter is that the calling is used for the benefit of the community. "A vocation or calling is a certain kind of life ordained and imposed by God for the common good."[30]

Secularism often tries to disguise the religious roots of capitalism in this country or deny the divine calling of its practitioners, but those roots can still be discerned in its many exhortations and convictions. The most celebrated capitalist in American history, Benjamin Franklin, provides Weber with a good case in point. Even though Franklin rejected some of the specific tenets of Puritan faith and might appear secular on the surface, his concept of capitalism was clearly shaped by his religious upbringing. He was reared in New England by devout parents of Puritan persuasion and educated as a boy in their schools. This upbringing certainly had a lasting impact on his life, because much of his thought and energy display a pious devotion to those teachings. Franklin conceived capitalism in terms of the ethical and religious aphorisms in which he was educated. It is these ethical norms that have utilitarian value and make one "healthy, wealthy, and wise."

His calling to make money is clearly in concert with the moral exhortations he received as a boy. One hears the same exhortations to frugality, temperance, diligence, and dedication to the community that we just witnessed among the Puritans. In accordance with his background, Franklin believed that money had great generative power if it was put to good use.

> Remember, that *credit* is money. If a man lets his money lie in my hands after it is due, he gives me the interest, or so much as I can make of it during that time. This amounts to a considerable sum where a man has good and large credit, and makes good use of it. Remember, that money is of the prolific, generating nature. Money can beget money, and its offspring can beget more, and so on. Five shillings turned is six, turned again it is seven and three-pence, and so on till it becomes an hundred pounds. The more there is of it, the more it produces every turning, so that the profits rise quicker and quicker.[31]

However, like a Puritan, capital can only be accumulated and employed by practicing certain austerities. The "way to wealth" is through "industry and frugality." Money cannot be wasted on "superfluities" or "expensive follies" like chinaware, fine clothes, Indian silks, etc. The goal of life is not to become rich or lead a bourgeois life-style but to be useful to the community through the productive use of capital. The individual only has a right to basic needs, and all else must be given away or put to good use in the community. Money cannot be wasted in this way, nor can it be wasted on leisure and idleness. Franklin considered idleness to be the deadliest of all sins, totally worthless to the betterment of oneself or society.

> Remember, that *time* is money. He that can earn ten shillings a day by his labor, and goes abroad, or sits idle, one half of that day, though he spends but sixpence during his diversion or idleness, ought not to reckon *that* the only expense; he has really spent, or rather thrown away, five shillings besides. . . . *Sloth, like rust, consumes faster than labor wears; while the used key is always bright,* as Poor Richard says. *But*

*dost thou love life, then do not squander time, for that is
the stuff life is made of,* as Poor Richard says. . . . *If
time be of all things the most precious, wasting time
must be,* as Poor Richard says, *the greatest prodigality;*
since, as he elsewhere tells us, *Lost time is never found
again; and what we call time enough, always proves
little enough.* Let us then up and be doing, and doing
to the purpose; so by diligence shall we do more with
less perplexity. . . . *Early to bed, and early to rise, makes
a man healthy, wealthy, and wise,* as Poor Richard
says. . . . *Diligence is the mother of good luck, and God
gives all things to industry. Then plough deep while
sluggards sleep, and you shall have corn to sell and to
keep.* . . . Leisure is time for doing something useful. . . .[32]

He rejected any attempt by the government to subsidize
the poor or even raise the minimum wage. Such measures
would only encourage laziness.[33]

Benjamin Franklin also exhibited the spirit of his Puritan background in his well-known passion for science. His
interest in science displayed a practical or utilitarian approach—all-so-typical of Puritanism. His many inventions—
the Franklin stove, bifocal lenses, the lightning rod, etc.—
attest to his interest in practical application. His faith in the
progress of science is also related to his Puritan roots. He
had the same millenarian expectation that one day it will be
possible to cure or prevent all diseases, lengthen our years
beyond current standards, and lighten our work load through
the advance of technology.[34]

Most people do not identify scientific interest with religious concern, but this attitude only demonstrates the power
of secular forces to suppress the role that religion plays in
culture. These people often refer to specific incidents where
conflict arose between scientists and religious authorities—
the papacy's condemnation of Galileo or the Fundamentalists' denunciation of Darwin. But few sociologists today,
especially after the work of Robert Merton, would deny the

intimate relationship between religion and science, both in its origin and present day practice.

Merton was one of the first practitioners of the sociology of science in this country, and he also was one of the first to show the importance of Puritanism to the evolution of modern science. There are few today who would dispute his findings in any substantive way. A simple examination of the leading figures of science at its birth during the seventeenth century reveals that many of them were clerics of Puritan persuasion, and the ones who were mere laymen, like Robert Boyle and Isaac Newton, pursued science with the same sense of religious mission. Puritans were "the dominant element in the scientific community, and they were responsible for the great bulk of the scientific publications." Take, for example, the famous Royal Society of London, which was dedicated to improving society through experimental science. Dorothy Stimson states that the leading figures and founders of the society were either divines or eminently religious men and that 62 percent of the original 1663 fellows whose religious backgrounds are known, had clear Puritan sympathies. The society was dedicated to the experimental method of research and practical application of scientific knowledge. Like all good Puritans, they valued no knowledge that did not have a solid use or service to humanity. In the Second Charter of 1663, which is still in effect today, the society found its purpose in "promoting by the authority of experiments the sciences of natural things and of useful arts, to the glory of God the Creator, and the advantage of the human race." While Puritans did not constitute a simple monopoly in the society or the field, their influence proved most essential in extending the discipline to other religions and communities. It was during the time of the Puritan Revolution (1640-1660) that the esteem of science began to grow dramatically.[35]

Francis Bacon, the great apostle of the scientific method, serves as a most illustrious example of the merger between religion and science. Bacon was the guiding light of the

Royal Society and the Puritan community in the philosophy of science. Bacon's writings came to have almost canonical authority among them. The experimental and utilitarian approach to natural philosophy was relatively unknown at the beginning of the seventeenth century, and it was through the writings of Bacon and those of like-mind that this approach came to the forefront of society by the end of the century.[36]

A major impetus for his belief was the distaste he shared with all Puritans for the idle speculations of the schoolmen in the Middle Ages. He said that the true end of scientific activity is "the glory of the Creator and the relief of man's estate." Life must be fulfilled as a participant in the community, not a spectator, and our knowledge should be concerned with what is useful. It should not engage in vain speculations or disputes to delight a "natural curiosity and inquisitive temper." Learning that is overly concerned with "the delicacy of language" or becomes "curious in things of little use" does not yield substantial results.[37]

It is because of these religious concerns that Bacon trumpeted the need for experimental science as a means of checking unbridled, rhetorical questions. Experimental control, not logic or poetry, is needed to produce an effective study of this world. The human mind should limit itself to what is feasible rather than entangle itself in "cobwebs of learning," which are not controlled by the substantial world of matter around us.[38]

Bacon follows the spirit of the Reformation in all this. He condemns those who attempt to probe the mysteries of God in nature rather than depend upon divine revelation in Scripture. (Luther and Calvin could not have made this case more forcefully.) The secrets of God cannot be found in nature apart from the "spectacles" of Scripture. The job of natural philosophy or physics must be consigned to answering mundane questions of secondary causality rather than finding the final cause of all things, which is beyond our purview and acumen.

And this was not only done by Plato, who constantly anchors upon this shore; but by Aristotle, Galen, and others, who frequently introduce such causes as these: "The hairs of the eyelids are for a fence to the sight. The bones for pillars whereon to build the bodies of animals. The leaves of trees are to defend the fruit from the sun and wind. The clouds are designed for watering the earth," etc. All which are properly alleged in metaphysics; but in physics are impertinent, and as remoras to the ship, that hinder the sciences from holding on their course of improvement, and introducing a neglect of searching after physical causes.[39]

By concentrating the methods of science no longer on metaphysical issues, science could now be free to reflect on simple problems and practical concerns, which it could solve with some certainty or at least make some progress toward a solution. Science need not answer grand, metaphysical questions of ultimate concern but will prove beneficial in answering simpler questions for the advancement of the community. It should limit itself to what it could do best and leave more sublime concerns to matters of faith.[40]

The Puritans reflected much of Bacon's point of view in their philosophy of education. They developed in the seventeenth century an iconoclastic disdain for classical education with its love for speculative, impractical subjects—subjects like philosophy, language, literature, and especially poetry. They preferred subjects like science and math, which were more useful to the progress of the community and more substantial in their reference to the spatiotemporal world of objects. The "serious employment of words" was connected to the world of real things or empirical-historical events. For a statement to have practical meaning, it must correspond to the tangible world of concrete reality and make a difference in it; and the same is true of education. It also must reflect this empirical, pragmatic orientation. Science and prose are preferred to fanciful flights of imagination as a more substantial and productive way to appropriate the good things of the world. Mathematics, chemistry, physics, and vocational studies are the preferred avenues of study.[41]

Puritans believed that their method of education would lead to a societal and intellectual rebirth in England. They combined the concept of social amelioration with a belief that real progress is possible in the world of ideas. They spoke of a "Great Instauration" (a world renewal) in which all social ills could be mitigated. In Bacon's *Magna Instauratio*, science would help lead the way. It had the potential to master the environment, exploit its material resources, and create a better world for our children. Their favorite verse of Scripture was Dan. 12:4. The prophet Daniel says that, in the latter days, "many shall run to and fro, and knowledge shall be increased." The prophecy of running to and fro was being fulfilled in their day and age by the expansion of commerce and navigation, including the discovery of the New World. The increase in knowledge was being fulfilled through the expansion of scientific and practical interests. Speculative disputes were giving way to more certain and useful concerns, which would yield quantifiable, incremental results. The future looked bright. "Experimental medicine could solve the problems of disease; agricultural innovation could restore the plenty of a Garden of Eden." The fall of humanity in the Garden was not an irreversible judgment of God, but has commissioned us to labor all the more, so that we might reverse its devastation and renew the dominion that we once enjoyed over nature (Gen. 1-3).[42]

> And as Man is thus by Light restord to the dominion over his own house, soe, by Magnalias that are brought to light, Hee is restored to a dominion over all the beasts of the field, over the birds of the ayre & over the fishes of the Sea. Here you must adde the discovery of, or dominion over all the Workes of God; the conversion of Stones into Metalls & backe againe; of poisons into powerful Medicines, of bushes,

thornes & thickets into Wine & oyle, & of all the
Elements to take such guise as Man by divine
Wisdome commands.[43]

America became the great experiment for this ideology.
The religious ideals of Puritans and other dissident groups
became woven into the fabric of the American culture. The
government was based upon their congregational polity. The
laws were designed to protect what God had given to all in
nature. The culture worked to build a better tomorrow. The
people invested their capital in the community and invented
technological marvels to enhance their lives. America became the greatest testimony to the power of Puritan ideals.
Its institutions, laws, customs, and beliefs were infused with
the spirit of their Puritan forefathers—the spirit of democracy and liberty, capitalism and pragmatism, individual rights
and natural law. America came to believe that it had a
special destiny to fulfill in bringing these ideals to fruition
and creating a better world for the rest of humankind. The
prophecy of John Winthrop was fulfilled. "We shall be as a
City upon a Hill, the eyes of all people are upon us. . . . We
shall be made a story and a byword through the world."[44]

What is so surprising today is how ungrateful and for-
getful the nation has become toward its spiritual moorings.
There seems to be a concerted effort to suppress its spiritual
roots and promote the willful ignorance of religious concern
in its present-day ideals. Our public schools in particular
have become protagonists of spiritual ignorance and secular
falsehood. At one time, the nation's textbooks interpreted
its history and vision in terms of religious passion,[45] but
today's textbooks would create the impression that the early
colonists wished to emancipate themselves from religion and
live by their own secular wits. Robert Bryan says,

> *These textbooks are written to propound the thesis that
> America was settled for the sake of religious freedom, and
> that religious freedom means the absence of religion* [em-
> phasis in original]. . . . Once the [early Eastern sea-
> board] settlement has been effected, and the popula-

tion has escaped from the trammels of religion, religion need not be mentioned again. There are exceptions to this general rule, but they are so sporadic as
to be incapable of conveying anything like the true
importance of religion in America. . . .[46]

Paul Vitz claims in an exhaustive study that most of the
nation's social studies and history texts have little or no
reference to the significance of religion and its motivations
in American life. If religion is mentioned at all, it refers to
certain antiquated beliefs of two hundred years ago or some
eccentric, minority view in the present day (e.g., the Amish).
The public schools generally ignore the religious motivations of the founding fathers in forging the nation's beliefs
and marginate its ongoing influence in our lives today. Vitz
blasts the public school system for preaching ignorance and
excluding "the history, heritage, beliefs, and values of mil-
lions of Americans."[47]

William Nord also claims in his study of standard textbooks that religion is for all practical purposes ignored or
entirely absent.[48] He does not find a massive conspiracy
behind its exclusion but believes that the net effect of failing
to mention its role teaches a secular view of the world,
regardless of the motive. It creates an atheistic impression
when God or religion is left unmentioned and so made
irrelevant to what one studies or addresses. He contends
that those who advocate the exclusion of religion from our
textbooks in the pretext of neutrality would not find the
exclusion of African-Americans and females so innocuous.[49]

The motivation of those who wish to exclude religion is
varied. Some wish to be sensitive to minority religious expressions and reduce offense. Others wish to separate religion from culture as irrelevant to our secular or public lives.
The former come under the banner of multiculturalism, and
the latter under the veil of separation between church and
state. But regardless of their motivation, the exorcism of
religion from culture is impossible. No culture or society is
formed without religious concern. Can one separate

Shintoism from imperial or present-day Japan? Can one separate Hinduism from the hierarchical nature of Indian society? Can one separate Islam from the socialistic designs of Arab nations? Can one separate Puritanism from the American system of government?

The fact is that the founders of our country were Christians, that this religion still remains dominant today, and that the country cannot help but reflect its image. The doctrines upon which the country was established remain a vital force in its existence and cannot be separated from its present nature. Even if the secular culture no longer identifies itself with the Christian past, it is clear that much of American ideology received its initial inspiration from specific religious concerns. This, of course, does not mean that other religious communities have not made a vital contribution to the culture; nor does it mean that all our ideology must be credited to one religious source. One could write an account of the Jewish, Catholic, Baptist, or Quaker contributions to the American way of life. While we have chosen to speak of the Puritan influence as most obvious and essential, the basic point is that religious motivations play a vital role in society and culture regardless of their identity. The vision, purpose, and morals of a society are intimately connected to its religious concerns, and America serves as a supreme example of this influence.

Notes

1. A. M. Adams and C. J. Emmerich, *A Nation Dedicated to Religious Liberty: The Constitutional Heritage of the Religious Clauses* (Philadelphia: University of Pennsylvania, 1990), 26; S. L. Carter, *The Culture of Disbelief* (New York: Anchor Books, 1993), 99; T. C. Reeves, *The Empty Church: The Suicide of Liberal Christianity* (New York: The Free Press, 1996), 39.

2. *The Collected Works of Abraham Lincoln*, ed. R. P. Basler (New Brunswick, NJ: Rutgers University Press, 1953), 6.155-156.

3. J. Dunn, *The Political Thought of John Locke* (Cambridge: University Press, 1969), x-xii, 259, 263.

4. J. Locke, *Concerning Civil Government, Second Essay*, in *Great Books of the Western World*, ed. R. M. Hutchins (Chicago: Encyclopaedia Britannica, Inc., 1978), 56. Cf. *Ibid.*, 25; E. C. Gardner, "John Locke: Justice and the Social Compact" *Journal of Law and Religion* (1992), 349-350; Dunn, *The Political Thought of John Locke*, 11, 97.

5. *Ibid.*, 53.

6. *Ibid.*, 25-36.

7. *Ibid.*, 25-26.

8. J. Locke, *A Letter concerning Toleration* (*Great Books of the Western World*), 12-15.

9. *Ibid.*, 1, 4, 8, 10, 15, 20.

10. *Ibid.*, 14; Dunn, *The Political Thought of John Locke*, 99.

11. A. Harnack, *Militia Christi*, transl. D. Gracie (Philadelphia: Fortress Press, 1981), passim.

12. *D. Martin Luthers Werke* (Weimar: Herman Böhlau, 1883-), 11.267; 12.331; 36.385; *Works of Martin Luther* (Philadelphia: Muhlenberg, 1930), 5.39; H. Oberman, *Luther: Man between God and the Devil*, transl. E. Walliser-Schwarzbart (New Haven and London: Yale University Press, 1989), 47-49, 66-68; J. Stayer, *Anabaptists and the Sword* (Lawrence, Kansas: Coronado Press, 1972), 36.

13. J. Calvin, *Institutes of the Christian Religion*, ed. J. T. McNeill, transl. F. L. Battles (Philadelphia: The Westminster Press, 1975), 4.11.11-14; 20.1-3, 9 (1223-1226, 1485-1489, 1495).

14. C. J. Dyck, "The Suffering Church in Anabaptism" MQR 59 (1985), 5.; *The Legacy of Michael Sattler*, transl. and ed. J. H. Yoder (Scottsdale: Herald Press, 1973), 40; *Anabaptism in Outline: Selected Primary Sources*, ed. W. Klaasen (Scottsdale: Herald Press, 1981), 23, 85, 244, 267, 290-292. The Quakers, Anabaptists, and German Pietists will forge a "holy experiment" in the Delaware Valley, where religious pluralism, liberty of conscience, minimal

government, and egalitarianism (even between the sexes) will flourish. D. H. Fischer, *Albion's Seed: Four British Folkways in America* (New York and Oxford: Oxford University Press, 1989), 429-430, 461, 490ff., 498, 568-569, 597, 819.

15. *The Writings of James Arminius*, transl. J. Nichols and W. R. Bagnall (Grand Rapids: Baker Book House, 1977), 2.136-137, 148, 479, 508-509; *Acta Synodi Nationalis* (Dordrecht: Isaac Ioannid Canin, 1620), 1.395; P. Limborch, *A Compleat System, or Body of Divinity*, transl. W. Jones (London, 1702), 37-39, 908, 911, 970, 983, 999-1005.

16. J. Cotton, *The Doctrine of the Church* (London, 1644), 1, 12; *The Way of the Churches of Christ* (London, 1645), 56, 61-64, 102-103; *Of the Holinesse of Church Members* (London, 1650), 24; W. Walker, *The Creeds and Platforms of Congregationalism* (Boston: Pilgram Press, 1960), 8, 13, 29, 69, 106, 116, 144-145; *Cambridge Platform* (in *The Creeds and Platforms*), IV, 3, 4; VI, 1; VIII, 5-7; X, 3; XVI.

17. *Cambridge Platform*, IV, 3, 4; X, 5. Puritans felt that their government is subject to a covenant of the people—well before Thomas Jefferson and the other so-called "Founding Fathers" of this country. The government is limited by the compact, subject to the rule of law, and dependent upon the will of the people. The people even possess the right to rebel against any magistrate who would violate their trust. P. Miller, *The New England Mind: The Seventeenth Century* (Cambridge: Harvard University Press, 1963), 409-410. For a history of the religious origin of covenant or federal theology see C. S. McCoy and J. W. Baker, *Fountainhead of Federalism: Heinrich Bullinger and the Covenantal Tradition* (Lousiville: Westminster/John Knox, 1991).

18. A. de Tocqueville, *Democracy in America* (New York: Alfred A. Knopf, 1963), 1.32, 39. Cf. *Ibid.*, 1.56, 59, 61, 81. The notions of a "general parish meeting" and a "general town meeting" were one and the same among the Puritans. These notions have antecedents in East Anglia, a stronghold of Puritan sentiment in England, and were transplanted into America. D. H. Fischer, *Albions' Seed*, 196. For an illuminating discussion of Virginia's Anglican polity, aristocratic government, and patriarchal society see D. H. Fischer,

Albion's Seed, 207ff., 234-235, 278-280, 298-300, 314-315, 358, 384, 399, 408ff.

19. Christianity brought a more peaceable and humane way of dealing with our fellow man. Christ told his disciples to love their enemies, pray for those who persecute them, and turn the other cheek to those who strike them. He felt that the kingdom of heaven was destined for those who are meek and merciful, poor in spirit and lowly in heart, makers of peace and lovers of righteousness. When Christians came to dominate the Roman empire the collapse of its despotic and imperialistic designs was inevitable. The people no longer possessed a religion or heart that would proselyte this type of kingdom. In America, Christianity helped to shape a country that sought peace in the world rather than worldly dominion, even though it obtained the military strength to do otherwise. Its designs were shaped by its religious ideals and would have been much different if it had followed another (more warlike) religion. Montesquieu, *The Spirit of the Laws*, transl. and ed. A. M. Cohler, B. C. Miller, and H. S. Stone (Cambridge: Cambridge University Press, 1997), 5. 24. 3ff., 14 (461ff., 468-469). Cf. *The Koran*, transl. N. J. Dawood (Middlesex, England: Penguin Books, 1974), 2: 216; 8: 37ff.; 9: 1ff.; 58-60; J. Kelsay, *Islam and War* (Louisville: Westminster/John Knox Press, 1993), passim; C. E. Lincoln, *The Black Muslims in America* (Boston: Beacon Press, 1961), 78, 116, 123, 152-153.

20. *Manifesto of the Communist Party* (in *Great Books of the Western World*), 416, 419-420, 424-428; R. L. Heilbroner, *The Worldly Philosophers* (New York: Simon and Schuster, 1961), 119-120.

21. Tocqueville, *Democracy in America*, 2.20.

22. *Ibid.*, 1.31-32, 43-44, 300-301, 306-307, 320-322; R. Novak, *The Spirit of Democratic Capitalism* (New York: A Touchstone Book, 1982), 15-17, 351. Of course, the Puritans did not live up to our present ideals in these and other matters, but they did provide a matrix from which further development did come. The influence of Puritans does not depend upon their complete conformity to our ideals. After all, influence never walks on all fours.

23. M. Weber, *The Protestant Ethic and the Spirit of Capitalism*, transl. T. Parsons (New York: Charles Scribner's Sons, 1958), 36,

44, 91; R. Green, *Protestantism and Capitalism: The Weber Thesis and Its Critics* (Boston: C. Heath and Co., 1959), vii; W. Hudson, "Puritanism and the Spirit of Capitalism" (in *Protestantism and Capitalism*), 62; H. M. Robertson, "Criticism of Max Weber and his School" (in *Protestantism and Capitalism*), 80-81; E. Fischoff, "The History of a Controversy" (in *Protestantism and Capitalism*), 109.

24. C. Webster, *The Great Instauration: Science, Medicine and Reform—1626-1660* (New York: Holmes & Meier Publications, 1976), passim; Weber, *The Protestant Ethic*, 59-60; Novak, *The Spirit of Democratic Capitalism*, 38-39. Societies that follow tradition and worship ancestors are sentenced to live in the past.

25. R. Baxter, *A Christian Directory: Or, A Summ of Practical Theologie* (London: Robert Write, 1673), 1.131; 2.448-450; iv. 147; *The Work of William Perkins*, ed. I. Breward (Appleford, Abingdon, and Berkshire: The Sutton Courtenay Press, 1970), 446-449, 456; Weber, *The Protestant Ethic*, 17-18; "The Author defines his Purpose" (in *Protestantism and Capitalism*), 2; G. Poggi, *Calvinism and the Capitalistic Spirit: Max Weber's Protestant Ethic* (Amherst: University of Massachusetts Press, 1983), 40, 60; E. Troeltsch, "The Economic Ethic of Calvinism" (in *Protestantism and Capitalism*), 25; R. Tawney, "Religion and the Rise of Capitalism" (in *Protestantism and Capitalism*), 50-51; K. Fullerton, "Capitalism and Calvinism . . ." (in *Protestantism and Capitalism*), 8.

26. A. Smith, *An Inquiry in the Nature and the Cause of the Wealth of Nations* (New York: The Modern Library, 1937), 320-321.

27. Baxter, *A Christian Directory*, 2.632; 4.143, 147; *The Workes of the Famous and Worthy Minister of Christ, . . . M. William Perkins* (Cambridge: Iohn Legatt, 1613), 125(B), 128(D), 134(A), 135(B); *The Work*, 453, 462-466; Fullerton, "Capitalism and Calvinism," 16-19; Troeltsch, "The Economic Ethic," 23-24; Hudson, "Puritanism and the Spirit of Capitalism," 58-60, 63.

28. *Ibid.*, 1. 65, 134, 274, 448; 2.632; 4.146-147; Perkins, *The Work*; Weber, *The Protestant Ethic*, 157, 172.

29. Weber, *The Protestant Ethic*, 112, 153; S. Strehle, *The Catholic Roots of the Protestant Gospel: Encounter between the Middle Ages and the Reformation* (Leiden: E. J. Brill, 1995), 34; Fullerton, "Capitalism and Calvinism," 9-12; Poggi, *Calvinism and the Capitalistic Spirit*, 65. For John Locke's discussion on labor, calling, and utilitarianism, see Dunn, *The Political Thought of John Locke*, 222, 251.

30. Perkins, *The Work*, 446-449; Baxter, *A Christian Directory*, 1. 132; H. M. Robertson, "A Criticism of Max Weber," 71; R. H. Tawney, "Religion and the Rise of Capitalism," 51-52; Weber, *The Protestant Ethic*, 79-80, 178-179; *The Sociology of Religion*, transl. E. Fischoff (Boston: Beacon Press, 1964), 220.

31. *The Works of Benjamin Franklin*, ed. J. Sparks (Boston: Tappen and Dennet, 1844), 87-88.

32 *Ibid.*, 87, 95-97.

33. *Benjamin Franklin's The Art of Virtue: His Formula for Successful Living*, ed. G. L. Rogers (Eden Prairie, MN: Acorn Publishing, 1986), 159, 162-164; *Benjamin Franklin: Writings* (New York: The Library of America, 1987), 345, 1082; *The Works*, 86, 90, 98, 368-371; *Reappraising Benjamin Franklin: A Bicentennial Perspective*, ed. J. A. Leo Lemay (Newark: University of Delaware Press, 1993), 443; Weber, *The Protestant Ethic*, 48; K. Fullerton, "Calvinism and Capitalism," 7; H. M. Robertson, "A Criticism," 82.

34. *Writings*, 1017, 1167; I. B. Cohen, "The Science of Benjamin Franklin," in *Critical Essays on Benjamin Franklin*, ed. M. H. Buxbaum (Boston: G. K. Hall & Co., 1987), 138, 143, 148.

35. D. Stimson, "Puritanism and the New Philosophy in Seventeenth-Century England," in *Puritanism and the Rise of Modern Science: The Merton Thesis*, ed. I. B. Cohen (New Brunswick and London: Rutgers University Press, 1990), 153-155; R. Merton, *Science, Technology & Society in Seventeenth Century England* (New York: Howard Fertig, 1970), 32-35, 112, 122, 128, 134-135; Webster, *The Great Instauration*, 88, 92-95, 116, 491, 496-497, 504; Cohen, "Introduction: The Impact of the Merton Thesis," in *Puritanism and the Rise of Modern Science*, 14, 69; A. de Candolle, "The Influences of Religion on the Development of the Sciences"

(in *Puritanism and the Rise of Modern Science*), 146; S. F. Mason, "The Scientific Revolution and the Protestant Reformation," in *Puritanism and the Rise of Sciences*, 185.

36. Merton, *Science, Technology & Society*, 88, 94-95, 105-106; R. F. Jones, "The Advancement of Learning and Piety," in *Puritanism and the Rise of Modern Science*, 164-165, 169; T. K. Rabb, "Puritanism and the Rise of Experimental Science in England," in *Puritanism and the Rise of Modern Science*, 211; Webster, *The Great Instauration*, 54-56, 61, 99, 514.

37. F. Bacon, *Advancement of Learning* (New York: The Colonial Press, 1899), 8, 14; Merton, *Science, Technology & Society*, 64-65, 72-73, 93; "Motive Forces of the New Science," in *Puritanism and the Rise of Modern Science*, 118; P. Miller, *The New England Mind: The Seventeenth Century*, 100ff.; *The New England Mind: From Colony to Province* (Cambridge: Harvard University Press, 1962), 408-409, 418.

38. *Ibid.*, 15-17, 21, 137; Webster, *The Great Instauration*, 189.

39. *Ibid.*, 97.

40. *Ibid.*, 18, 95, 213-214; Webster, *The Great Instauration*, 22, 44, 336.

41. R. Merton, *Science, Technology & Society*, 17-19, 118-123; Stimson, "Puritanism and the New Philosophy," 151; R. A. Nibet, *History of the Idea of Progress* (New York: Basis Books, Inc., Publishers, 1980), 131; Webster, *The Great Instauration*, 199.

42. Webster, *The Great Instauration*, 2, 29-30, 44, 325-388; Nibet, *History of the Idea of Progress*, 129, 195-198; Merton, *Science, Technology & Society*, 230; S. F. Mason, "The Scientific Revolution and the Protestant Reformation," 184.

43. Letters from Beale to Hartlib (15 September 1657 and 26 March 1659), in Hartlib Papers, Sheffield University Library as quoted in Webster, *The Great Instauration*, 328.

44. J. Winthrop, "A Modell of Christian Charity Written on Board the Arabell, On the Atlantick Ocean," Winthrop Papers (The Massachusetts Historical Society, 1931), 2.295.

45. R. M. Elison, *Guardians of Tradition: American Schoolbooks of the Nineteenth Century* (Lincoln: University of Nebraska Press, 1964), passim; F. Fitzgerald, *America Revised* (New York: Vintage Books, 1980), 75-76.

46. R. Bryan, *History, Pseudo-History, Anti-History: How Public School Textbooks Treat Religion* (Washington, DC: Learn, Inc. The Education Foundation, 1984), 3, 10.

47. P. Vitz, *Censorship: Evidence of Bias in Our Children's Textbooks* (Ann Arbor, Michigan: Servant Books, 1986), 14-16, 39-41, 58-59, 75-78. Vitz, a professor of psychology at New York University, was funded by the government (NIE) to examine bias in textbooks. He examined "ninety widely used elementary social studies texts, high school history texts, and elementary readers" to arrive at his conclusion.

48. Nord analyzes forty-two high school textbooks, written from 1989-1992 and used by his state of North Carolina, in the areas of American and world history, economics, home economics, biology, physics, and physical science. All these texts are published by major publishers and represent standard works used nationwide. Similar studies by Timothy Smith, Paul Gagnon, and even the People for the American Way arrive at the same conclusion. T. L. Smith, "High School History Adopted for Use in the State of Alabama: The Distortion and Exclusion of Religious Data," *Religion and Public Education* 15 (Spring 1988); P. Gagnon, *Democracy's Untold Story: What the World History Textbooks Neglect* (Washington, DC: Education for Democracy Project, 1987); T. Podesta, "The Uphill Battle for Quality Textbooks," *Religion and Public Education* 13 (Summer 1986), 60-62.

49. W. A. Nord, *Religion and American Education: Rethinking a National Dilemma* (Chapel Hill and London: University of North Carolina Press, 1995), 69, 139ff., 190, 197. Even the Supreme Court has warned the state about establishing a "religion of secularism." *Abington v. Schempp*, 374 US 203, 225; *Torcasa v. Watkins*, 367 US 488, 495n.

CHAPTER II

Reason, Morals, and Faith

God confronts us everywhere in life—originally, immediately, and first of all. The whole universe is His sanctuary, and nothing can escape from the presence, the omnipresence, of His divine nature. Whether we descend to the depths of Sheol or retreat into the innermost chambers of the heart, God is there to lay hold of us (Ps. 139). The heavens are His throne; the earth His footstool (Isa. 66:1). There is no place to hide. There is no space that He does not fill with His presence. No matter how mundane, no matter how secular, there is nothing that can escape the true and proper ground of its being. Every person is a temple of His Spirit. "Every work day is a day of the Lord, every supper a Lord's Supper; every work a fulfillment of a divine task, every joy a joy in God."[1]

Paul Tillich was fond of saying, "God is the ground of all being." By this he wished to emphasize that all of life— its truth, goodness, beauty, et al.—is dependent upon the existence of God as the true and proper ground of all being. For Tillich, all we hold dear in life would have no ultimate meaning, significance, or reference without God. There would be nothing to which these concepts refer, nothing ideal or absolute. There would be no reason for us being here beyond mere chance, no explanation for what occurs beyond happenstance, no standard for us to strive after, no purpose for us to fulfill, and no meaning behind our everyday, temporal affairs—at least nothing of ultimate concern. We would simply be here by accident, and life would have no ideals or goals to lend it purpose. We would be subject to matter—a blind, chaotic, and capricious matter, and there would be no way to explain it or anything else outside the irrational nature from which it arose. There would be no God to provide matter with intelligibility or orchestrate the discord into a grand unity. We would have no metaphysical foundation to believe in life's fundamental rationality, or justify our present life as meaningful, or create a new life and order that would conform to some ideal standard. All would be meaningless. All would be striving after the wind. And all of us would need to confess what the philosophers know all too well: "If God did not exist, all things would be permissible" (Dostoevski); "If God did not exist, it would be necessary to invent him" (Voltaire).[2]

Reason

The most important philosopher of the modern era, Immanual Kant, saw belief in God much along these lines. His account is especially important, since he above all will set the agenda for the place of God in the modern world. His belief in God is demanded by the same rational concerns that we have seen above. God is an assumption that reason must make in order to justify its program. Theoretical reason seeks to find the ultimate, unconditional cause of it all in the midst of an endless chain of events, which provide only secondary answers of limited concern. Practical reason seeks to establish a basis for morality and the good life *(summum bonum)* in a world that seems so indifferent to those who long for justice and a better world.

In the *Critique of Pure Reason*, Kant begins his discussion of the subject wondering whether it is possible to speak of any metaphysical object, let alone God, since such an object resides outside our field of vision and there is no proof of its existence. A metaphysical object is that which subsists "beyond nature" by definition, and would appear to be out of sight and out of mind for those who are limited to an empirical world—i.e., a world that is limited to five senses only. Kant wants to afford a critique of our reason in his work and find out whether it can transcend the empirical objects of this world—what we see, taste, and touch—and continue to speak of that which lies beyond. Can reason support belief in a metaphysical object like God? Can reason speak of His nature as if God were an object of knowledge? The *Critique of Pure Reason* was written to answer these questions and show the limits of what reason can and cannot do.[3]

The answer that Kant provides in his work must be viewed in the final analysis as *sic et non* (yes and no). At first, he rejects all talk of proof for the existence of God, whether classical arguments or future arguments. He believes that one could literally argue out of both sides of the mouth and never resolve the antithetical thoughts that occur in its discussion. If one was limited to mere speculation, one would vacillate a lifetime over the alternatives without approaching a solution or glimmer of light. However, he does not stop here. He goes on to say that faith is still necessary. Its necessity arises not so much from this speculative mode of reason and its equivocations but from the interests that reason has in general to justify its own agenda. In other words, reason believes in God because it wants to. Reason is not a dispassionate observer of life pure and simple but has appetites that want to believe in the fundamental unity or rationale of what is observed, even if it must go beyond the data to assume what it cannot see or prove. Its propensity is to unify. Its natural disposition is to synthesize the series of conditions in this world as much as possible, and so it must assume that such a project is possible. It must assume that there is a fundamental unity and rationale to what it studies; otherwise it would be spinning its wheels and wasting its time.[4]

It is out of this need to provide a basis for the use of reason that Kant offers a number of metaphysical ideas as essential to us. Of these ideas, three are particularly brought forth and listed as most essential to the quest.

The first concerns the belief that we all share in the "unity of the thinking subject" (i.e., the ego or "I" lurking behind all that we think, say, and do). There is no direct empirical evidence of the ego. We cannot see it or touch it, and yet in our daily intercourse we continually speak of it and assume its existence. It becomes a necessary assumption of ours, because we cannot explain without it how our various ideas could be coordinated together in any other manner. Thinking, acting, smelling, feeling, etc. seem to require a locus or subject from which they could be engendered and coordinated. We could not identify our thoughts or activities without a unified self-consciousness, nor could we hold others responsible for their acts without it and say, "*You* are the man." A unity of self-identity must be assumed to coordinate our thoughts and deeds together, even if it cannot be seen directly with our senses.[5]

The second idea that Kant puts forth concerns the belief in the "unity of the series of conditions." This belief proposes that the diversity of the natural forces around us can be brought together into an intelligible, systematic whole or, in accordance with the Latin term *universus*, "turned into one." The data, of course, remain incomplete, but Kant felt that there is simply no reason for a physicist to get out of bed in the morning if the series of phenomena in the world could not be made ultimately intelligible. There would be no reason to continue. The goal of physics is to provide a fundamental explanation of life in material terms, and it is incumbent upon its practitioners to assume the existence of a universe, even if it cannot be seen as a whole or demonstrated through any current theory or analysis.[6] After all, if there is no universe, then there is no unified field theory out there; if there is no unified field theory, then nature must be left to its own irrational forces, defying all attempts at explanation.

The final idea casts its shadow over the previous two as the "unity of the condition of all objects of thought." It is here that Kant reaches the highest expression of systematic unity with his belief in a Supreme Being, who is "necessary" and "unconditioned." With this idea, reason is provided with what it wants most, an ultimate explanation for it all. Such a Being would be independent of the series of conditions in this world and provide it with a sufficient reason for its existence as the beginning and end of all. There could be nothing more that reason wants—a final and sufficient answer to life's questions. Life would present more than a simple rendition of what happens to transpire. It would serve some purpose within the counsels of an all-wise and all-knowing deity.[7]

Even tragedies could be explained beyond the scientific and clinical responses of the conditioned world. Certainly, explaining to a mother whose child just perished in an avalanche the series of conditions—alternating temperatures, melting snow, refrozen water, expanding ice, and loosened snowbank—does not bring much comfort or satisfy reason. A mother wants to know what purpose this tragedy serves in the ultimate scheme of things. She wants to believe that God's will has been done or some ultimate purpose has been served by what seems, from all appearances, to be a senseless tragedy. It is because of this that reason first posits the existence of God. While it cannot see God or perceive the answer so simply, it must continue by its very nature to search for an answer, an ultimate answer, to whatever life presents it.

Of course, there are many in the academic community who are quite sceptical about all this, especially in the realm of physics. The debate covers all disciplines and pervades all times, but it is the physicists who present the most decided challenge in the present context.

The atomists of ancient Greece are considered the patriarchs of the atheistic side of the debate in physics. They believed, much like their counterparts today, that life could

have evolved out of the simple, interactivity of matter, even
if matter is blind and irrational in itself. According to their
theory, life consists and only consists of what they called
"atoms" *(atomoi)*—numerous, invisible particles of various
shapes and sizes—and these atoms are eternally in motion.
This motion is particularly important because it is through
motion that the atoms can come into contact with each
other and interact. Even if they are blind and stupid and
have no senses to perceive each other, they can still interact
or interlock when happenstance causes them to collide and
form the shapes and sizes that we see around us. It is through
the mere chance of a collision that clusters are formed, objects
are fashioned, and the worlds evolved into their present
states.[8]

The atomists have convinced many philosophers and
scientists down through the ages of the validity of their
thesis. In the ancient world, the Epicureans spoke of the
"first-beginnings" in much the same way—eternal, indestruc-
tible, and infinite, separated by a vast void, and always in
motion. They rejected the notion that divine intelligence
could have guided the first-beginnings into their current
station in life, mainly because of the inexplicable nature of
human suffering. The misery of this life does not bespeak of
divine providence or a wise creation but is more compatible
with the chaotic motion, violent collisions, and fortuitous
combinations of a senseless origin.[9]

In more recent times, a number of physicists have employed the powerful techniques of modern science to defend
this theory, even if many of its experiments remain stranger
than fiction, if not totally unintelligible. The experiments
show electrons acting as a particle when observed and as a
wave when they are not observed, protons cognizant of each
other's spin even at a distance, and radioactive decay emitting and not emitting particles in a random, unpredictable
manner. These strange phenomena seem so much at odds
with our daily experience and have engendered a number of
varied interpretations as one can imagine. The most famous

is the so-called Copenhagen interpretation, which contends for the fundamental irrationality and capriciousness of these particles. "The world is governed by the accumulation of outcomes of essentially random 'choices' of possibilities at the quantum level." While its particles might not be so blind as the atomists once thought, the same fundamental commitment to chaos is plainly in view.[10]

On the other side of the debate, the most oft-quoted response to this analysis must be attributed to the great physicist, Albert Einstein. He is noted for dismissing quantum theorists with the simple quip, "God does not play dice." Einstein, in the name of God and reason, could not accept the results of what he considered a stopgap measure (Shrödinger's equations) to a problem that would eventually require a more coherent explanation. Even though he was a cofounder of quantum theory, he could not accept its results and later became one of its most incessant critics.

He preferred instead to follow the likes of Baruch Spinoza, a most religious-minded philosopher and rationalist. Spinoza had looked at life as a product of the divine nature (i.e., absolutely necessary, completely determined, and utterly rational; so much so that he bordered on pantheism, the belief that God is all, in many of his writings). Einstein found inspiration in these writings and displayed the same tendencies toward Spinozan rationalism through his own identification of the universe with the divine nature, as well as his lifelong pursuit of a unified field theory that would combine all of life's forces into a grand, rational whole. Any talk of irrationality and chance was simply out of the question.

Of course, this response is nothing new. It has a long history that stretches back through many distinguished philosophers, theologians, and physicists of the past. The road, in fact, goes all the way back to ancient Greece, where rational theism received its initial impetus, and especially to Aristotle, who provided its most classical form. It was Aristotle and his concept of causality that provided the basic outline for subsequent treatments of God and the nature of the world. No other treatment, not even Einstein's, has superseded its place in the history of theism.

Aristotle did not believe that a material cause is sufficient to explain the world, just as it is not sufficient to explain the multiplicity of causes and effects that we experience in our everyday lives. For example, in order to build a house, more is needed than wood, nails, bricks, and mortar (the material cause). One also needs a carpenter to do the hammering and a mason to do the laying (the efficient cause), an architect to draw up a blueprint that will form and fashion the material and direct the activity (the formal cause), and a family whose needs set the purpose for the project or determine all the rest (the final cause). The world, he says, is no different from this or any other mundane case. It displays order *(cosmos)* and purpose *(teleos)* much like the objects of human craft and therefore requires the same sort of final cause that would set its agenda, too. Brute matter does not constitute a cosmos. It cannot fashion itself into the wondrous forms and complex shapes that are found in the world at large. Only God could provide the basis for this orchestration and design, and true wisdom must never be satisfied until it arrives at the final or ultimate cause to which all other knowledge is subordinate. True wisdom does not limit itself to the baser means of life but the "first causes and the principles of things; so that, as has been said before, the man of experience is thought to be wiser than the possessors of any sense-perception whatever, the artist wiser than the men of experience, the master-worker than the mechanic, the theoretical kinds of knowledge are to be more of the nature of wisdom than the productive."[11]

To illustrate this theory, let us consider the origin of eyesight. A typical, atheistic explanation for its origin is found in the following comments by Lucretius:

> To interpret these or any other phenomena on these lines is perversely to turn the truth upside down. In

> fact, *nothing in our bodies was born in order that we might be able to use it, but the thing born creates the use.* There was no seeing before eyes were born, no talking before the tongue was created. The origin of the tongue was far anterior to speech. The ears were created long before a sound was heard.[12]

Lucretius wishes us to believe that the eye was not designed by some antecedent force to see, but came into existence by chance and only discovered a use later. But is this possible? "Does He who planted the ear not hear? Does He who formed the eye not see?" (Ps. 94:9) Can that which is blind fortuitously construct a complex mechanism like an eye without recognizing what it is looking for? Can matter blindly go about its business and construct complex senses as if by chance? It would seem unlikely, at least *prima facie.* It would be like constructing a television set without expecting a picture!

Darwin tries to explain the origin of the eye by pointing to possible precursors (e.g., tiny creatures who have pigmented cells that are light sensitive). Stephen J. Gould, a Harvard paleontologist, speculates that the eye could have evolved out of intermediate structures, which changed their function along the way. But Michael Behe, a biochemist from Lehigh, complains that the Darwinian model does not account for the molecular structure of the eye. He says that Darwin's gradual, step-by-step process does not account for the biochemistry of the eye or the many other "irreducibly complex machines" that make up the body. The cell itself was a black box to Darwin, and its numerous, complex operations unknown. These operations—cilium, blood clotting, the immune system, intracellular transport, etc.—consist of numerous interconnected chemicals, all of which are necessary for their function and all of which have no other purpose. Behe says that he did a computer search to find an article, paper, or book that affords a Darwinian explanation of these systems and found nothing—nothing but pure bluster.[13]

Regardless of whether one finds this argument compelling or not, the basic point remains unaffected. The purpose of the discussion is not to be found in a defense of either side of the debate, but in a recognition of what must be admitted by all, that God and reason are related in a fundamental way and do not exist apart from each other. It is indeed possible, if not likely, that the theists are wrong about their belief in God. Most of them would admit that their faith is no more than an assumption that is posited to meet certain existential needs. It could be true, as Feuerbach and Freud contend, that religion is nothing more than a neurotic fairy tale created by wishful thinking people and that the theist needs to grow up and admit, "Man is what he eats." But there is one thing that appears to be most certain for us all—a truth that the big babies of atheism must grow up and face themselves—not that God exists, but that life would not contain one scintilla of meaning without Him. This is our conclusion, and we make no concession on this point. Life, if it is to have any reason whatsoever, must spell that reason with a capital *R*.

If one chooses to reject God, one must also be prepared to live with the ramifications of that choice. It might be much easier to reject all reason and all divine truth in theory than to live without these principles in the real world. There are many postmodernists who have made that choice and are more than willing to trash all reason for the sake of power in the world of academia, but outside their ivory tower it is indeed questionable whether such a philosophy has much practical value in our everyday lives. Can one live without reason? What would be the basis of our relationships with each other or our society as a whole if life was relegated to power plays? How could we adjudicate our differences or come to agreement? How could we even communicate with each other?

Jürgen Habermas says that those who dispense with reason have also dispensed with the only mechanism for social integration. Society needs a mechanism by which it can build consensus, coordinate its actions, and unify the people with a binding force, and that force can be none other than reason. It is reason that allows us to escape our own provincial world and recognize what we share in common with others. In order to come together and coordinate our actions, we must be able to understand each other. Bias must give way to what is valid, prejudice to mutual understanding, and power to rational agreement.[14] There must be an answer to our problems or at least a better way to proceed, based upon right reason or the laws of nature (John Locke). Otherwise, we would exist in a natural state of radical individuality and power plays, where chaos and war would be the norm and might would determine what is right. Tyranny, the exercise of great power, would be its only, possible outcome (Thomas Hobbes).

While Habermas does not invoke the name of God, he does speak often of a logic that transcends local contexts and has universal validity. This notion has clear theistic implications, even if he does not admit it. Habermas would rather limit his discussion to concrete forms and avoid the speculative Idealism of Hegel and his Absolute Spirit, but one wonders whether any substantive difference really exists in the final analysis, other than points of emphasis. Perhaps God is not so politically correct as He once was in Hegel's day. But, whatever the reason, Habermas speaks of the universal and absolute Logos (Reason) as the basis of society, and this is what we call God. For Habermas, society is based upon an absolute and ideal use of reason that can adjudicate our differences and determine what is valid. For us, society is based upon God, and the idea of a secular society must be considered an oxymoron.[15]

Morals

However, it is not reason but morality that reveals God's presence to us most directly in society. In morality, one cannot help but speak of that which is transcendent and ideal by its very nature. Because of this, Immanuel Kant considered morality to be the very heart of religion. "Moral-

ity thus leads ineluctably to religion, through which it ex-
tends itself to the idea of a powerful moral lawgiver, outside
of mankind, for Whose will that is the final end (of creation) which at the same time can and ought to be man's
final end." Kant believed this so strongly that he tended to
reduce religion to morality, rejecting all other matters—grace,
miracles, prayer, confessions, ceremonies, etc.—as superflu-
ous to its essential nature or "pious play things and inac-
tion." "Religion is the recognition of duties as divine
commands. . . . The one true religion comprises nothing but
laws."[16]

Whether one agrees or not, it cannot be doubted that
Kant's moral philosophy had a profound influence on the
nineteenth century, as well as on many liberals today. No
matter how overstated, the relationship between morality
and religion is shown by him to be essential. Anyone who
wishes to divide the two hereafter has probably not considered Kant's analysis in all its gravity or the nature of morality and its clear, religious implications. Certainly in the post-
Kantian world, it is difficult to sustain a division between
the two under philosophical analysis, even if many of our
institutions for political reasons have chosen to do so.

In his *Critique of Practical Reason*, Kant attempted to
show how those who wish to think and live in a moral way
must postulate the existence of God as its necessary basis.
Of course, it is possible to live a moral life without God in
accordance with the dictates of practical reason, but such a
life would not be consonant with the nature of morality and
its implications. The main reason offered by Kant for his
position concerns the belief that we all have about the *summum bonum* or highest good (i.e., a life filled with both
virtue and happiness). A synthesis between the two is demanded by our reason, but it is difficult to demonstrate this
so simply. All of us recognize, deep down, that virtue should
have its rewards, but we cannot prove that this is so through
analytical reason, and through our experience in the empirical world, there is much that seems to be the opposite.

"There is futility that occurs on the earth, that is, there are righteous men who get what the wicked deserve and wicked men who get what the righteous deserve. I say that this is futile" (Eccl. 8:14). Kant believed that those who thirst for righteousness must postulate the existence of God to rectify this matter. A harmony between virtue and happiness cannot be expected if life consists and only consists of simple, causal events, so indifferent to moral concern. Only a God who is above this world and possessed with moral passion could possibly affect a reconciliation. The moral life demands it and we must assume it, if our deeds are to possess ultimate validity. We must assume a divine reconciliation between virtue and happiness and a fulfillment of the moral life, whether it be in this world or the one to come.[17]

In a later work, *Religion within the Limits of Reason Alone*, Kant expanded upon his discussion and speaks of God as a "Holy Legislator," whose will is written in our hearts and whose commands become the basis for moral law. This line of argument is particularly interesting, although Kant's discussion of it is not so inspiring as his earlier work. So it might prove more fruitful to compose a generic argument, which draws upon a number of sources, instead of following Kant's treatment specifically. The argument will still be consonant with Kant's fundamental belief that the existence of God must be assumed for the sake of morality, but the specific reasons will be altered.

The first reason that we offer concerns the standpoint from which moral judgments are wrought. When one speaks from a moral point of view, one brings judgment to bear on a matter of concern. This judgment does not simply describe what it sees and hears but expresses pleasure or displeasure in accordance with some standard. Without this standard, there would be no basis to pass judgment, only an account of the way things happen to be. Moral judgment believes in something ideal or absolute, a standard worthy of that name. Otherwise, it could not continue with its program. And so, it must believe in God. It is God and God alone who allows morality to speak, because it is He and He alone who provides it with an ideal and absolute standard of perfection. There is no other vantage point. All else would be caprice. Morality declares what is ideal and absolute and brings that standard to bear in its attempt to create a better world. It speaks of God and from God by its very invocation, and apart from God it must be condemned to silence.

This is why the knowledge of God is so fundamental to a society. It sets the standard by which all acts must be judged and all citizens must live. Plato, in his Republic, did not want Homer's *The Iliad* and *The Odyssey* taught to the citizens (*hoi polloi*) because its depiction of the gods as quarrelsome and lecherous would corrupt the knowledge of the Good and lead to moral laxity. Moses, when he set before the children of Israel their societal laws, began on the first tablet by prohibiting false gods, false images, and the misuse of the name of God, and only afterward did he speak of the people's relationships one to another. In the New Testament, this example of God becomes incarnate in Christ, as Christians become known as disciples or followers of Christ.

> In this the love of God was manifested among us, that God sent His only Son into the world that we might live through Him. In this is love, not that we loved God but that He loved us and sent His Son as an atoning sacrifice for our sins. Dearly Beloved, since God so loved us we also ought to love one another. (1 John 4:9-11)

The second reason why the existence of God is needed concerns the standpoint from which moral judgments are rendered. Moral judgments come from an ideal vantage point which exists above and beyond this world. They are synthetic and metaphysical in nature, which means that they cannot be constructed from simple, sensible data. A scientist could never discover what is right or wrong through microscopes or telescopes. The development of a fetus from conception to delivery might be described in copious, biological detail, but moral questions that concern its worth cannot be addressed at all. While science can provide data in its own, special way, which guide those who make informed decisions, it cannot render any moral parameters by which the final choice is made. All moral choices are transcendent in nature. They speak from a divine perspective. They do not speak of the world as it "is" but bring some ideal perspective from another dimension to bear on the situation and declare what "ought" to be. They do not describe the world; they judge it. It is only from this ideal state—transcendent, metaphysical, and heavenly—that they can bring their judgment to bear.

Of course, there are some who try to promote moral concerns without invoking the name of God, but none of them appears to satisfy rigorous philosophical analysis. J. S. Mill proposed an ethical system (utilitarianism) that would identify what is good with that which we desire or produces pleasure. "The sole evidence . . . that anything is desirable is that people do actually desire it."[18] However, most philosophers ridiculed this proposal and accused him of committing the "naturalistic fallacy" (i.e., mixing the good with nature or what we ought to desire with what we do in fact desire). What we desire could include all sorts of perverted things. John Searle tried to go in another direction and demonstrate that some value judgments could be descriptive and not metaphysical. In the case of a promise, he thought that there is an implicit obligation, intrinsic to its nature, that it ought to be fulfilled, although he later admitted that the entire institution of making a promise could be questioned.[19] G. E. Moore engaged in the vacuous double-talk of saying, "The good is the good." He said that it is incapable of definition and can only be perceived *prima facie*—immediately, self-evidently, and intuitively. His answer was to provide no answer.[20]

Max Weber said in a famous passage that no one today attempts to establish values through the use of reason except "a few big babies." Allan Bloom in *The Closing of the American Mind* cites this passage and finds that most of these big

babies seem to reside in America, where rationalism has
been ascendant for some time. John Dewey, the patriarch of
American education and pragmatism, serves as a most illustrious example of one who wants the whole American
dream—naturalism and moralism, relativity and values. Out
of one side of his mouth, we are told that life is nothing
beyond a continuous stream of change and has no purpose
or end-in-view but that which we fix, arbitrarily, out of our
own likes and dislikes. Life in itself serves no purpose and
has no meaning. Out of the other side, we are told that
common experience can create an "inherent standard of
judgments and values" from nature, even though he never
delivers these values or bothers to explain how this is done.
In the end, we are left with the same vacuous claptrap we
heard before, "Values are values, things immediately have
certain intrinsic qualities. Of them as values there is accordingly nothing to be said, they are what they are. All that can
be said of them concerns their generative conditions and the
consequences to which they give rise."[21] Dewey for all his
bravado remains enclosed in his own series of conditions.

A more sober-minded analysis is presented by the atheistic existentialist, Jean-Paul Sartre, in his popular work
Existentialism and Human Emotion. He, unlike his American counterparts, seems to confront the tragedy of his atheism, at least in this work, head on. He admits that all ethical
ideas disappear if God does not exist and "man is condemned to be free"—free to do anything. Sartre is willing to
face "all the consequences" of his atheism and chides his
own fellow countrymen who would try to create a secular
ethics in the absence of God as just another version of
Weber's "big babies."

> When we speak of forlornness, a term Heidegger
> was fond of, we mean only that God does not exist
> and that we have to face all the consequences of this.
> The existentialist is strongly opposed to a certain
> kind of secular ethics which would like to abolish
> God with the least possible expense. About 1880,

some French teachers tried to set up a secular ethics which went something like this: God is a useless and costly hypothesis; we are discarding it; but, meanwhile, in order for there to be an ethics, a society, a civilization, it is essential that certain values be taken seriously and that they be considered as having an *a priori* existence. It must be obligatory, *a priori*, to be honest, not to lie, not to beat your wife, to have children, etc. So we're going to try a little device which will make it possible to show that values exist all the same, inscribed in a heaven of ideas, though otherwise God does not exist. In other words—and this, I believe, is the tendency of everything called reformism in France—nothing will be changed if God does not exist. We shall find ourselves with the same norms of honesty, progress, and humanism, and we shall have made of God an outdated hypothesis which will peacefully die off by itself. The existentialist, on the contrary, thinks it very distressing that God does not exist, because all possibility of finding values in a heaven of ideas disappears along with Him; there can no longer be an *a priori* Good, since there is no infinite and perfect consciousness to think it. Nowhere is it written that the Good exists, that we must be honest, that we must not lie; because the fact is we are on a plane where there are only men. Dostoievsky said, "If God didn't exist, everything would be possible." That is the very starting point of existentialism. Indeed, everything is permissible if God does not exist, and as a result man is forlorn, because neither within him nor without does he find anything to cling to. He can't start making excuses for himself. If existence really does precede essence, there is no explaining things away by reference to a fixed and given human nature. In other words, there is no determinism, man is free, man is freedom. On the other hand, if God does not exist, we find no values or commands to turn to which legitimize our conduct. So, in the bright realm

of values, we have no excuse behind us, nor justification before us. We are alone, with no excuses. That
is the idea I shall try to convey when I say that man
is condemned to be free. . . .[22]

While Sartre never retracts his existentialist philosophy,
he, like many atheists, found it difficult to live in full accord
with its principles. It is one thing to create a philosophy,
another thing to live it; and atheism has particular problems
in this regard. After all, it is difficult to live in the real world
without some involvement in its ethical and social concerns.
Sartre himself did not escape these concerns. He is noted for
his participation in the French resistance to Nazism in World
War II and supporting the Communist Party after the war,
for his condemnation of France's "unjust" and "dirty" war in
Algeria, and excoriating the American government for its
bombing of Hanoi; all of these actions speak of ethical concern.

Yet, we should not be too harsh in our criticisms of
these inconsistencies. Sartre was man enough to admit them,
at least on certain occasions, and none of us who live within
the tensions, twists, and paradoxes of life can present to
others a full, systematic unity of it all, whether in word or
deed. Bertrand Russell, another atheist and activist, admitted the same.

> I am accused of inconsistency, perhaps justly, be-
> cause, although I hold ultimate ethical valuations to
> be subjective, I nevertheless allow myself emphatic
> opinions on ethical questions. If there is an inconsis-
> tency, it is one that I cannot get rid of without in-
> sincerity; moreover, an inconsistent system may well
> contain less falsehood than a consistent one. . . . In
> the first place, I am not prepared to forego my right
> to feel and express ethical passions; no amount of
> logic, even though it be my own, will persuade me
> that I ought to do so. There are some men whom I
> admire, and others whom I think vile; some political
> systems seem to me tolerable, others an abomina-

tion. Pleasure in the spectacle of cruelty horrifies me, and I am not ashamed of the fact that it does. I am no more prepared to give up all this than I am to give up the multiplication table.[23]

Faith

The power of reason to discuss ethical and other metaphysical issues, independent of God and His revelation, has been greatly diminished in the modern world. Its current status is certainly much in contrast to the more exalted position that reason enjoyed at the origins of philosophy in ancient Greece, even though there have always been Cynics, Sceptics, and Sophists to disparage its powers.

Socrates, the first of the great philosophers, was concerned mainly with ethics and its dissemination, which he hoped to establish through his own rational faculties. He was concerned with establishing definitions of ethical categories that were universal and absolute, and hoped to instill their truth into his pupils, as well as the Athenian citizenry. Just as one can teach a medical student to use medicine, so one can teach a student of ethics how to be just. Education is the panacea. It can answer our questions categorically and create model citizens, too. Socrates became so enthralled with the benefits of his knowledge that he went on to equate virtue and knowledge. He believed that one who knows what is right will do what is right. In the *Republic*, he made the bold statement that education safeguards against tyranny, and a properly educated ruler would insure the creation of an ideal state. Thus there is born the tradition of a philosopher-king.[24]

Aristotle extended the program of Socrates and Plato, his mentor. While he did not equate virtue and knowledge, he did believe in the ability of the intellect to discover the truth, the whole truth, through its inductive and deductive powers. His books cover a wide range of subjects: ethics, metaphysics, politics, rhetoric, poetry, physics, astronomy, botany, etc., and his discussions became the standard for the next two millennia.

The church became the guardian of culture after the Greeks and wrestled with the relationship between its revelation of God in Christ and the wisdom that it received from Greek philosophy. The answer to the problem is difficult and varied. Some see reason as compatible with faith; others see it as totally opposed. Some see it as subordinate to faith; others view reason as basically autonomous. Justin Martyr, a second century apologist of the church, essentially merged the two. He spoke of God in both Aristotelian and Christian terms and Christ as the *Logos* (Reason). Tertullian, a third century theologian, proceeded in the opposite direction and denounced all philosophers as the "patriarchs of heretics." He cried, "What is Jerusalem to Athens?," and contended that faith must stand on its own merit over and against the objections of reason. Augustine in the fifth century and Anselm in the eleventh century represented a more centered approach as they considered reason an important means of explaining the faith but clearly wished to subordinate its power to faith. "They did not believe because they understood, but they believed in order that they might understand." Thomas Aquinas, the angelic doctor of the thirteenth century, bestowed on reason a more autonomous role than Augustine or Anselm as he became particularly enthralled with the writings of Aristotle, whom he called "the philosopher." Reason is said to have its own special dignity in nature, apart from faith, even if faith is still needed to complete what is lacking. It is through the likes of Thomas that Aristotle gained ascendancy in the Middle Ages and became a dogma that rivaled any church creed. In the late medieval period, even God could not defy the logic of Aristotle. It was said among the theologians of the day that God could do almost anything through His absolute power except violate Aristotle's law of contradiction.

Modern philosophy will begin its history by debunking all previous authority, especially Aristotle's, but it will continue to entrust itself to the power of reason. René Descartes wished to "sweep away" all that went before him, doubted everything he believed, even his own existence, and placed philosophy upon a more rational and solid footing. His ideal system of philosophy was constructed in accordance with a mathematical (geometric) model, by which he hoped to develop self-evident axioms, deduce other principles, and construct a complete "rational scheme" of indubitable truth. His first truth is the famous *cogito*. "I think, therefore I am."[25]

Montaigne also manifested this new spirit of modern philosophy by rejecting the all-sufficient authority of Aristotle. He rejected this authority not because he wishes to contest the value or certainty of its content, which is good and edifying, but in order to exhort its followers to expand their horizons and recognize a variety of ideas and truths. He felt that life contains too many twists and contradictions to be limited by one perspective or to be captured by a simple, systematic presentation of its mysteries. His orientation was much more eclectic than Descartes'.[26]

The eighteenth century witnessed the zenith of reason's power during the Enlightenment and was rightly called the Age of Reason. The object of wrath this time was not Aristotelian philosophy, but the dogma of the church. After two centuries of orthodoxy, where Catholic, Lutheran, and Reformed confessions of great detail were inculcated among the faithful and not-so-faithful, many decided to leave the authority of the church and the Bible behind and branch out on their own. The admonition of the day was to use your own mind. "Don't be a child and trust church dogma. Dare to know!" And so, the great era of natural religions began. Western culture would no longer trust in the revelation of God in Christ, but ventured out from the church and used its own reason to ascertain first principles, the existence of whatever ultimate power there might be and whatever duties are necessary to perform.

There are many examples that could be used to illustrate this philosophy, but none can compare, at least for our purposes, to Thomas Paine, the irrepressible gadfly of the

American Revolution. It was his pamphlet "Common Sense" that helped incite the colonists to revolt against their mother country and his book *Age of Reason* that presented the most politically incorrect account of Enlightenment philosophy. He started out by proclaiming, "My own mind is my own church." His faith was said to be "deducible by the action of reason upon the things that compose the system of the universe." Through our reason, we can contemplate divine power in the immensity of creation, divine wisdom in the eternal laws of nature, and divine mercy in the abundance that is supplied to us daily. Paine drew on the typical analogy of the day. He compared the universe to a "great machine" and believed that it required an intelligent designer or what he called "the great mechanic" to explain its mechanism. No rigorous philosophical argument is presented beside this, and little theological development is found. His faith is simply in one God, whose moral character should be imitated, and the possibility of an afterlife in which wickedness will receive some punishment.[27]

As far as revealed religion is concerned, he considered it most wicked and most irrational. He called the Bible "a book of lies, wickedness, and blasphemy." It is filled with stories of rapine and murder, including the "horrid assassination of whole nations." It inspires "the most detestable wickedness, the most horrid cruelties, and the great miseries that have afflicted the human race." He called the Jews "a nation of ruffians and cut-throats," their patriarchs "monsters and imposters," the Apostle Paul a "fool," and Christians "infidels to God." The wicked deeds of these wicked men are what the Bible offers us, and beyond this, there is little else other than stupidity. No enlightened mind could possibly believe in its mythological and miraculous stories, or its mystical doctrines such as the Trinity and the divine incarnation, which defy all logic. What person of intelligence could accept such an account? And even if it was credible, how can we trust in a revelation of bygone days, which was given to others and we did not experience personally? Each of us possesses the wherewithal to find God for ourselves in creation, and we, as good stewards should use it accordingly. "The creation is the Bible of the true believer."[28]

If the eighteenth century produced the zenith of reason's arrogance, it also planted the seeds for its eventual undoing in the modern world. Its excesses invited a reaction, as one might expect, and the reaction was strong. At the end of that century, there appeared two important philosophers who disparaged the ability of reason to prove much of anything and set considerable limits on what matters it can and cannot entertain. They, above all others, determined the place of reason in the modern world.

The first of these philosophers is David Hume, the Scottish sceptic from Edinburgh. Hume is particularly noted for his discussion of the problem of reason and causality. It is his contention that our conclusions concerning cause and effect are founded upon our experience and are not subject to rational understanding. We do not know in advance that a stone which is raised in the air and then left without any support will fall to the ground. There is no reason that can prove this or demonstrate why such an event has occurred. Any so-called explanation through occult entities like gravity represents nothing beyond pure, scientific mystification. It is only custom, habit, and experience that allows us to expect its fall to the ground. "Causes and effects are discoverable, not by reason, but by experience." We do not know that direct contact with fire will harm us until we stick our hands in a flame. We do not know whether the sun will rise in the morning until we wake up and see. There is no intuition or demonstration that could indicate what will happen in advance. We cannot examine an object and determine what caused it or what kind of effects it will produce. It is not our reasoning that perceives what objects and events are associated together, but it is experience and experience alone that can inform us of what transpires.[29]

Hume applied his scepticism to many areas of life, but for our purposes none exceeds the significance of his unrelenting assault upon proofs for the existence of God. Among the numerous arguments that are related in his works, the argument from the nature of causality is considered the most important. In common life, Hume argued that a cause cannot be known simply from its effect, as we have just seen. This problem of causal argumentation only multiplies when we attempt to transcend our experience and speak of the nature of the universe and its cause. It is difficult to argue from cause to effect or effect to cause in our everyday life, how can we possibly speak about the origin of a universe of which we only know a small part or a Supreme Being who is so superior and so remote to anything with which we are familiar? It is dubious enough to argue this way in common life, let alone in regard to matters of which we have no analogy. The universe might not be like a house (Aristotle) or a machine (Paine) as the proponents of these proofs would say, but more like some organic process, which scatters its seed and vegetates into new worlds. But who knows? It is certain that we were not there at the origin of the world to experience its cause, and without this vital experience our reason is not able to speculate over what could have caused it. "Where were you when I laid the foundation of the earth, Tell me, if you understand. Who marked off its limits? Surely you know! Who stretched a measuring line across it?" (Job 38:4, 5).

Hume's diatribe against reason and its inability to demonstrate the existence of God should not be construed as an attack upon belief in God. He does not present his arguments to destroy faith. His scepticism has only sought to abase reason from the haughty position that it usurped during the Enlightenment and provide the first step toward faith in the revelation of God, which must look beyond the pale of human experience, custom, and reason. "A person, seasoned with a just sense of the imperfections of natural reason, will fly to revealed truth with the greater avidity.... To be a philosophical sceptic is, in a man of letters, the first and most essential step towards being a sound, believing Christian."[30]

The second of the philosophers who helped to dismantle the Age of Reason was Immanuel Kant. He, at one time, followed the teaching of the Enlightenment, especially his mentor Christian Wolff, but was awakened out of his "dogmatic slumber" by the work of Hume toward a new concept of reason and faith. As we have seen, his *Critique of Pure Reason* attempted to ascertain how far reason can go beyond experience and ask metaphysical questions. This criticism, Kant says, is a much more general and fundamental program than Hume's scepticism, which only points out specific fallacies in particular arguments of reason. Kant shows both the limits of what reason can prove in general and the need to assume metaphysical ideas like God in order to justify its program. Reason is seen to believe in God in spite of its inability to prove His existence on its own. This program will effectively destroy the Enlightenment's concept of reason as an autonomous entity and rival to faith. It need not be reiterated at this point, since it has been mentioned earlier in some detail. What needs to be underscored is the monumental role that it played in dismantling the haughty place that reason assigned to itself in the eighteenth century. Both Kant and Hume prostrate an arrogant reason, which would defy all trust in God, not to destroy metaphysics or reason, but to make room for faith. Their program will provide the basic outline for belief in God within the modern world.

The nineteenth and early twentieth centuries witnessed a number of revolts against the all-encompassing power of reason. Søren Kierkegaard, the father of existentialism, extolled the passions and cravings of the soul over against anything that reason could present. The life of a real individual cannot be placed into the straightjacket of some system of thought but involves passionate and fearless ventures into unknown, unchartered courses, which no amount of abstract thinking could predict or even help the individual in making. Sigmund Freud, the founder of psychoanalysis, viewed his patients as controlled by what resides deep within the psyche—unconscious ideas that have their archaic origins in childhood. The impulses of the unconscious or Id are considered much stronger than what lies on the surface or under our control, and psychoanalysis is needed to draw out the repressed thoughts and rectify the situation. Friedrich Nietzsche, the father of postmodernism, relegated all to power (the "will to power") and rejected all those who seek the truth through reason. What he wanted were "supermen," who do not submit to the petty norms of the masses or the illusions of reason but create their own truth and morality—a "master morality."

Today mainline philosophy has completely abandoned the interests of reason. The classical questions of the philosophical past are no longer even addressed. All metaphysical categories, which now include reason within its fold, transcend the limitations of what we can think about, and what we can think about is not thinking or morality or any other divine idea but simply the words that we use to express our beliefs. There is no thinking outside of language in the twentieth century, no higher criterion by which we could judge what is said; only words and more words, only talk and more talk are the subject of study.

Ludwig Wittgenstein provides the most important impetus toward the study of language in the twentieth century. In fact, much of philosophy today is divided between those who follow the early Wittgenstein in attempting to place language within overarching logical categories and those who follow the later Wittgenstein in seeing wonder and uniqueness within every sentence. While the differences are important, what concerns us here is more what the stages share in common. In all stages, language is considered the vehicle of thought, and its domain is limited to what is possible to discuss. His early work, *Tractatus*, sets the basic agenda. In it, he tries to limit what we talk about to the relationship of objects in this world. "The world is all that is the case." Anything outside this world that would lend it value—God or ethics—is considered off limits; even science with its laws of nature (e.g., causality) imposes alien forms which do not belong to our experience of this world. All metaphysical concepts defy the logic of language and produce nonsensical questions that can never be answered. The mission of philosophy is not to answer the riddles of life or even create propositions that command our acceptance, but to clarify what is thought and what cannot be thought clearly, "we must pass over in silence." His *Investigations* will go on to display the mental process (epistemology) as a mystery and the impossibility of tracing its steps. Knowledge is said to have no foundation. There is no thought or meaning or even discussion of the mental process outside of its expression in words, and no justification of its content. All we can do is display what we have to say through words—or maybe restate what we wish to say in other words if someone has any questions and hope the inquirer will see what we see. We cannot impart to him or her whatever insight we might have.

In his final work, *On Certainty*, Wittgenstein wrote that the reasons we list for what we believe are no more than various forms of subjective persuasion. Certainty is a subjective state that raises the intonation of the voice but cannot prove its assertions to ourselves or others. "What I know, I believe." And this belief does not speak with the authority or certainty of knowledge as if detached from our own inner state and offered in pure objectivity. It is offered merely and solely as an expression of our own subjective state of mind, which we cannot escape, no matter how strong we might feel about its assertions and no matter how much we might wish to convince ourselves or others concerning its veracity.[31]

"With the exception of professional rationalists, today people despair of true knowledge." These words of Albert Camus represent the malaise that has fallen upon many in the modern world. They recognize the plight of reason among Wittgenstein, Nietzsche, and all those who honestly confront its problems today, as well as the despair of many who now ask, what is the use? Camus, of course, is one of those who lived in despair and confronted the problem with all the sobriety and darkness of a French existentialist. He was even willing to ask, in light of the absurdity of life, whether suicide is not a viable option. If our striving has no purpose or leads to no result, what is the point of continuing? Camus compared us to Sisyphus, who was sentenced by the gods to roll a boulder up a mountain, watch it fall, and then begin another futile attempt to raise it, forever and ever. Why not just end it all? Why strive for what cannot be achieved? Camus does not provide a simple answer to his question. He does exhort us to continue the struggle, claiming that "something exceptional" is found in scorning our fate and enduring its absurdity, but it is hard to believe that even Camus could have been satisfied with his response.[32]

While the plight of reason has caused much anxiety in the secular world, the religious community often finds exultation in any debasement of autonomous, human abilities. Calvin wrote that we will not seek the good things of God unless we first become displeased with ourselves. Kierkegaard considered despair to be a necessary precondition for faith. Throughout this chapter, we have seen that a proper foundation for the rational and moral life is only found in God, and it is not surprising that those who live apart from God and trust in themselves find nothing of the divine image or the good things of God to follow. If God is gone, then so is all that we were created to be; gone, too, are all the reasonable solutions and righteous causes.

The plight of humankind in the twentieth century has brought about a revival of religious answers to life's questions. After the First World War, it became difficult for citizens to trust anymore in human perfectibility and progress, the great dogma of the previous century that now laid in ruin all around them. In the midst of the darkness of those days, a young preacher from the tiny Swiss village of Safenwil began to pronounce divine judgment upon liberal optimism as he turned his attention and that of the church back to the Scripture, especially its pronouncements in the book of Romans. The message particularly resonated in the hearts of those who were devastated by the depravity of human beings, and the young preacher went on to become the most celebrated theologian of the twentieth century. His name was Karl Barth, and his theology became known as crisis or judgment theology. He will serve our study as a most illustrious example of radical religious concern and our final appeal for the need for religion in this lost and fallen world.

The starting point in Karl Barth's theology is not human experience or its abilities, which must be brought to nothing, but a message that is the Lord's to grant and bestow, a message that he calls the Word of God. What we think and what we do must be set aside in order for God, and God alone, to speak. We do not possess in our own right a capacity to hear or discover the Word of God apart from God. There is no possibility of obtaining communion with God through our own sagacity and natural wit, as if we were capable of finding Him or manufacturing a religious experience on our own. There is nothing in our experience that generally or vaguely corresponds to God. He cannot be found as an object in this world for us to look outside and see. "In the cosmos God is hidden and man is blind." It is only divine initiative that can establish communion with those who reside outside His abode and only His grace that can heal those who share in the corruption of the world and dwell in darkness. God's Word would not be God's Word; His grace would not be His grace if there could be ascribed to human nature a predisposition toward the things of God. It is God's Word that finds and even declares us to be inadequate, and not only inadequate but totally corrupt and futile.[33]

For Barth, the Word of God is the only basis from which to speak. We cannot precede this Word. There are no higher criteria that we could erect as our standard and judge what comes from above. We cannot stand above the truth or prove the authority of that which is the standard of all truth. We do not know God apart from God, as if we could judge God to be God. He is the Lord. He is the truth. "Beside Him there is no other" (Deut. 4:35). It is His Word that encounters and judges us, and it is His Word that serves as the basis of our speech. It cannot be judged, defended, or established by any other means.[34]

This Word Barth identifies with the person of God, especially that Person as revealed in Jesus Christ. Revelation is not identified with an abstract idea to be placed in a creed, or a proposition to be memorized and recited, or a special law to be accepted and followed. It consists of neither creedalism nor legalism, but is found and only found in *Dei loquentis persona*, the person of God speaking. Even the Bible does not refer to itself but bears witness to Jesus Christ as the Word of God (John 1:1) and finds its fulfillment in this testimony. The power of the sign or witness of Scripture depends upon the activity of the divine Spirit, who must fill its letters with life and power, and the object of its testimony, who is none other than Jesus Christ. God does not hand His work over to another, even if that other is the Bible. "The Bible is *God's* Word." While the sign might become the arena in which God elects to reveal Himself, this can only transpire because it testifies to Him and the Lord has filled its testimony with His presence and meaning.[35]

And what is this testimony? It is certainly not what we would expect from our own devices. We would expect God in His revelation to be really great—like Cyrus the Great, Alexander the Great, or Herod the Great—one who would bask in grandeur and majesty, one who would dwell in regal splendor and dress in purple vestments, one who would sit upon a royal throne and issue imperial edicts to the plebes, one who would seek out, divide, and conquer (*veni, vidi, vici*). This is what we would expect and desire—a god who is the mere reflection of human arrogance and pride; pompous, austere, and imperious, dwelling in self-sufficient, self-centered narcissism, supreme imperial majesty and absolute transcendent glory; a god who looks very much like the devil.

However, the Word does not meet us in the form of glory but in the form of a servant and in the likeness of lowly human weakness (Phil. 2:6, 7). Scripture says that Christ had no stately form or majesty that we would look upon Him, nothing in His appearance that we should aspire after Him (Isa. 53:2)—no lustrous aureole, no regal vestures, and no kingly throne. In fact, the Word became an example of much the opposite of what our reason would expect; an example of patience, kindness, humility, and love; an example of One who did not assert His rights but yielded such judgment to Him who judges justly (1 Pet. 2:18); an example of One who did not regard His equality with God so important that He could not empty Himself and take the form of a servant (Phil. 2:5); an example of One who did not die for the righteous but the unrighteous—even His enemies (Rom. 5:8). This is contrary to what we would expect. The Jews expected a Messiah to destroy the Romans and exalt their nation above the rest. The Greeks expected God to remain enraptured above the misery and suffering of humanity in the world. Neither of them could find the revelation of God in the cross of Christ—a revelation that must crucify our preconceived notions and judge all our thoughts and ways.

> Where is the philosopher? Where is the scribe?
> Where is the debater of this age? Has not God made
> foolish the philosophy (*sophia*) of this world? For
> since in the wisdom of God the world through its
> wisdom (*sophia*) has not come to know God, God
> was well pleased through the foolishness of the mes-
> sage preached to save those who believe. Indeed the

> Jews ask for signs and Greeks search for wisdom, but
> we preach Christ crucified. This is a stumbling block
> to Jews and foolishness to Greeks, but to those who
> are called, both Jews and Greeks, Christ is the power
> of God and the wisdom of God. (1 Cor. 1:20)

These words of Paul are expanded in Collosians, where Christ is both the revelation of God and the very image unto which all things were created. "He is the image of the invisible God, the Firstborn of all creation . . . for through Him and unto Him all things have been created" (Col. 1:15, 16). This image becomes particularly identified with human nature as a vessel that is suited and fitted to bear that image—a vessel in which it will become incarnate. The union between God and man in Christ speaks of the original design and ultimate destiny for which we were all created. Paul says that we were created after the image of Christ (Rom. 5:14), renewed in that image through His Spirit (2 Cor. 3:18, Col. 3:10), and will be conformed to its likeness in the world to come (Rom. 8:29).

This means that God and man stand reconciled in Christ and, apart from this relationship, there is no understanding of what it means to be human. Our humanity certainly does not possess its own set of attributes and perfections apart from God as if it could be understood outside of that relationship. It does not possess its own autonomy, independent of the Creator, free to live in a secular world of its own fashion. Our image, the very essence of all that we were created to be, is found in communion with God, and apart from God we have no life, reason, or purpose. All that is good and righteous and true is found within the divine nature, and what goodness, righteousness, and truth we might exemplify in our lives can only come from the power of His grace. His goodness must become our goodness; His image our image. Any attempt to distance ourselves from God and live independently in our own power leads only to the destruction of our nature. There is no man without God. Adam is nothing but *adamah* (dust). His attempt to separate himself from God and possess a knowledge in his own right led only to his destruction.[36]

Notes

1. P. Tillich, *Theology of Culture* (New York: Oxford University Press, 1964), 26-27, 41; M. Buber, *I and Thou*, trans. W. Kaufmann (New York: Charles Scribner's Sons, 1970), 57, 128-129.

2. Tillich, *Systematic Theology* (Chicago: The University of Chicago Press, 1975), 1:11, 205-208, 237-239; *Theology of Culture*, 5ff., 42; S. Ogden, *The Reality of God and Other Essays* (San Francisco: Harper & Row, 1977), 35-36, 122-125. See W. Pannenberg, *Anthropology in Theological Perspective*, trans. M. J. O'Connell (Philadelphia: The Westminster Press, 1985), 472-474; P. L. Berger, *The Sacred Canopy: Elements of a Sociological Theory of Religion* (New York: Doubleday & Co., Inc., 1967), 33-36.

3. I. Kant, *The Critique of Pure Reason in Great Books of the Western World*, ed. R. M. Hutchins (Chicago: Encyclopaedia Britannica, Inc.), 4, 8-9.

4. *Ibid.*, 9, 112-113, 117, 119-120, 133, 192, 233.

5. *Ibid.*, 49-50, 89, 128. His *Critique of Practical Reason* emphasizes human freedom and responsibility.

6. *Ibid.*, 119, 160.

7. *Ibid.*, 178, 200. Cf. *Critique of Judgment*, trans. J. H. Bernard (New York and London: Hafner Publishing Co., 1966), 280-81, 287, 311.

8. *Metaphysics, The Basic Works of Aristotle*, ed. R. McKeon (New York: Random House, 1941), 985[b].

9. Lucretius, *On the Nature of the Universe*, trans. R. E. Latham (Great Britain: Penguin Books), 31ff., 51, 176ff. (I, 146ff., 803ff.; V, 170ff.).

10. J. Gribbin, *In Search of Schrödinger's Cat: Quantum Physics and Reality* (Toronto and New York: Bantam Books, 1988), 2-3, 120, 169-174, 203-205, 239-241.

11. *Metaphysics*, 981ᵇff., 993ᵇ-994ᵃ, 996ᵇ-997ᵃ, 1013ᵃ, 1072ᵇff.

12. Lucretius, *On the Nature of the Universe*, 156 (IV, 823ff.).

13. M. J. Behe, *Darwin's Black Box* (New York: Touchstone Book, 1998), 15ff., 22ff., 38-39, 82ff., 108ff., 136ff.; S. J. Gould, *Ever Since Darwin: Reflections in Natural History* (New York: W. W. Norton & Co., 1977), 103-104, 108. Gould admits that the gradual evolution of the eye is a problem for Darwinism.

14. J. Habermas, *The Philosophical Discourse of Modernity: Twelve Lectures*, trans. F. Lawrence (Cambridge: The MIT Press, 1993), 193, 281-282, 287, 314-315, 324; *The Theory of Communicative Action*, trans. T. McCarthy (Boston: Beacon Press, 1984, 1987), 1.86, 193, 287; 2.5.

15. *Ibid.*, xvii, 205; *The Theory of Communicative Action*, 1.1-2, 26, 31, 68, 137, 180, 219, 230; 2.195-196, 290.

16. I. Kant, *Religion within the Limits of Reason Alone*, trans. T. M. Greene and H. H. Hudson (New York: Harper & Row, Publishers, 1960), 5-6, 95, 142, 156, 182-183.

17. I. Kant, *The Critique of Practical Reason* (*Great Books of the Western World*), 291-292, 339ff.

18. *Mill's Utilitarianism*, ed. J. M. Smith and E. Sosa (Belmont: Wadsworth Publishing Co., 1969), 34, 61-62.

19. J. Searle, *Speech Acts: An Essay in the Philosophy of Language* (Cambridge: University Press, 1990), 182, 189.

20. G. E. Moore, *Principia Ethica* (Cambridge: At the University Press, 1968), 6-9.

21. J. Dewey, *Experience & Nature* (Chicago and La Salle: Open Court, 1994), 35, 84, 93-94, 303, 320-322, 348; *Reconstruction in Philosophy* (Boston: The Beacon Press, 1962), 70, 121, 180-181.

22. J -P. Sartre, *Existentialism and Human Emotions* (New York: The Wisdom Library, 1957), 21-23.

23. *The Philosophy of Bertrand Russell* (Evanston and Chicago: Northwestern University, 1944), 720.

24. *Republic, The Collected Dialogues of Plato*, ed. E. Hamilton and H. Cairns (Princeton: University Press, 1978), 415-416, 423ᶜ-424ᵃ, 472ff.; *Timaeus*, 86.

25. R. Descartes, *Meditations on First Philosophy* (*Great Books of the Western World*), 80-81, 103; F. Copleston, *A History of Philosophy* (Garden City, New York: Image Books, 1963), 4:95-97.

26. *Selections from the Essays of Montaigne*, ed. and trans. D. Frame (New York: Appleton-Century-Crofts, Inc.), 9-13, 16, 37, 41, 94-95.

27. T. Paine, *Age of Reason, The Complete Religious and Theological Works of Thomas Paine* (New York: Peter Eckler, 1954), 1:5-6, 29-31, 49, 67, 159, 185, 261-262, 307, 378, 415-416.

28. *Ibid.* 1:8ff., 18-19, 43, 60, 91, 103-104, 166, 173, 176, 249, 355-356, 398.

29. D. Hume, *An Enquiry Concerning Human Understanding* (Chicago: Henry Regnery Co., 1965), 24ff., 64.

30. D. Hume, *Dialogues and the Natural History* (Oxford and New York: Oxford University Press, 1993), 36-37, 46, 50, 53, 78-79, 84, 130; *An Enquiry*, 135ff., 147ff.

31. L. Wittgenstein, *Tractatus Logico-Philosophicus*, trans. D. F. Pears & B. F. McGuinness (London and Henley: Routledge & Kegan Paul, 1977), 3, 5 (1, 2, 2.01), 19 (4.003), 25-26 (4.112-4.1212), 56-57 (5.6-5.61, 5.632-5.633), 67-74; *Philosophical Investigations*, trans. G. E. M. Anscombe (New York: Macmillan Publishing Co., 1968), 103ff. (308ff.); *On Certainty*, ed. G. E. M. Anscombe and G. H. von Wright (New York: Harper & Row, Publishers, 1969), 24-26, 32-33 (245), 68 (520-521), 81 (612), 88 (669).

32. A. Camus, *The Myth of Sisyphus and Other Essays*, trans. J. O'Brien (New York: Alfred A. Knopf, 1969), 3, 9, 18, 21, 27, 40, 51-55, 77, 93, 119-123.

33. K. Barth, *Church Dogmatics*, I/1, 128, 220-223, 237-38; I/2, 26, 29-30, 41, 243, 249, 257; II/1, 87, 104, 182, 241-243.

34. *Ibid.*, I/1, 29-30, 42-43, 255-256, 259-261; II/2, 333, 400, 522, 537.

35. *Ibid.*, I/1, 109-113, 119, 136-138, 304; I/2, 223-225, 459-463.

36. Cf. Ibid., I/1, 144, 161-162, 194; I/2, 62-63; III/2, 15, 49-50, 71-72. We know of sin only in Christ. Ibid., IV/1, 7, 144, 360, 389, 400.

CHAPTER III

Secular Atheism

Atheism represents the final expression of those who view their life as existing apart from God. In its most literal form, it denies that God exists directly and categorically. The concept of God is considered a fabrication of wishful thinking, and the exhortation is to accept life as it is in all its brutal reality. There is nothing beyond this material world. There is nothing beyond the grave. In its subtler form, it does not make such dogmatic assertions but believes that life must go on without God, since He is beyond our limited field of vision. Bertrand Russell says that it is impossible to prove or disprove the existence of a being that transcends our experience in this world. He prefers to remain agnostic about the possibility and talk about other, more certain things. Ludwig Wittgenstein goes beyond Russell and wonders whether the question of God's existence is even meaningful. Since one cannot have a clear concept of what transcends us, the very question is considered unintelligible, or at least lacks sufficient clarity for the purposes of rigorous philosophical analysis. The word "God" does not refer to an object in this world and is therefore meaningless except in a religious or mystical way.

While these forms of atheism address important philosophical concerns, they are not as relevant to the present
concern as a more pervasive form that permeates popular
culture today. Jesus spoke of this type of atheism when He
ascended the Mount of Olives and characterized the days
before His second coming. He said that it will be just as it
was in the days of Noah, before the heavens opened and the
great flood poured forth its wrath. "The people," He said,
"were eating, drinking, marrying, and giving in marriage."
They had no thought of God or knowledge of the impend-
ing judgment. They were a-theistic and god-less. They lived
in their own secular world, carrying on its activities as if
God was simply irrelevant to the process, as if His gifts
could be received without grace. Christ says, "So it will be
in the coming of the Son of Man."

Paul expounds upon these words of Christ in 1
Thessalonians 5 and finds the same form of atheism to exist
in the latter days. He compares the coming of the Lord to
a thief who will surprise those enshrouded in the darkness
of their own security. He focuses upon the peace and safety
that the world will create out of its own devices and pro-
claim as its own, but this peace, he says, will not endure. He
exhorts us to disavow the promises of a secular world and
live with sobriety and vigilance, lest we forget the promises
of God. It is forgetfulness and secularity that concern Paul,
even more than a direct assault upon his message, because
in it God is left out of sight and out of mind. While direct
antagonism displays its concerns for the things of God
through opposition, secularity does not even bother or care.

This spirit becomes embodied in the rest of Scripture
within the tradition of the Antichrist. The Antichrist will
appear in the latter days to undermine the work of God, not
merely as an opponent to its purposes but as a substitute for
God Himself. "He will show no regard for the gods of his
fathers . . . Nor will he regard any god, but will exalt himself
above them all" (Dan. 11:37). Even his name is made to
speak of this mystery: the Greek prefix *anti* is often trans-

lated "instead of" in English, which indicates the vicarious or counterfeit nature of his designs, and the number of his name—666—is said to be that of man (Rev. 13:18). This means that the Antichrist represents the embodiment of godless man in all his secular glory as he presents himself as a substitute for Christ. It is in secularity that one acts independent of God, and it is the Antichrist who simply dispenses with God all together. In him it is not God who becomes man, but man who becomes God.

Western civilization has prepared the way for Antichrist in modern times. Secularism, humanism, and pragmatism mark the main forces that are ever-expanding their domain over all our lives. Its beginnings cannot be traced so definitively, but many would point to the "humanista" of fifteenth century Italy as providing an early inspiration for its current status. The humanists felt that some subjects such as rhetoric, grammar, poetry, etc. could be studied in their own right apart from any theological interest and thus represent an early manifestation of the modern secular spirit. While they did not wish to subtract religious concerns from the curriculum *in toto*, the burgeoning effect of these and other subjects did begin to preoccupy the mind of later generations and crowded theology from the exalted place that it enjoyed in the curriculum during the Middle Ages. Modern humanity, in fact, lost much of its theological moorings. Art became more interested in portraits and landscapes than religious scenes. Music began to exalt human love and eroticism. Science went on its fact-finding mission in the here and now. Business demanded technical and practical skills for the work place. Religion became less and less important and more and more sentenced to the fringes of society. Governments even passed laws to eliminate its influence from the public sphere.

In the eighteenth century, the French Enlightenment brought the process of secularization to the forefront with its anti-Christian and anticlerical agenda. The church had become by that time the object of much scorn for its beliefs and was blamed for all the ills that had befallen European civilization. High society found it most fashionable to ridicule Christianity as the religion of peasants and preferred to consecrate in its place the most irreverent and cynical writers of the day as spokesmen for its spirit. None of them was more beloved than Voltaire, the irascible and pugnacious man of letters and arch-hater of Christendom. Daniel Monet could say that Voltaire, near the end of his life, had become "Voltaire the God" in the affections of most Parisians.[1]

The contempt for the church in Voltaire and the French Enlightenment, while often overexercised, was certainly understandable within the context of those days. The Catholic Church had supplied its enemies with much ammunition. France, in particular, was reeling from Dominican inquisitions, Jesuit and Jansenist polemics, the massacre of Hugeunots on St. Bartholomew's day, and the revocation of the Edict of Nantes. The French government, during the last year of *l'Ancien Régime* (the Old Regime), employed 178 censors, who controlled publications and insured that reading material would be consonant with true religion, public order, and sound morality. Voltaire himself had certain of his works censored for deistic themes and was imprisoned eleven months in the Bastille for his avant-garde opinions.

It was in this context that Voltaire became the leading apologist in France for tolerance among all religious forms and ideas. He felt that his own country could profit from the example of Protestant countries who prospered under such a policy. He had been converted to this notion early on in his career through a visit to England, whose way of life impressed him, and the reading of its great intellectuals, especially John Locke. He went on to believe that all religious people—Muslims, Jews, Socinians, Catholics, Protestants, etc.—can live in harmony and practice tolerance one with another. They all practice the same essential virtues of good citizenship. They all worship the same Supreme Being, regardless of their doctrinal differences and priests who wish to emphasize the differences. He did not believe that true religion would divide humanity or stir up persecutions through speculative formulas and scholastic distinctions, which profit little. These speculations were ridiculous at best, and destructive at worst, when its priests try to coerce others to conform with their creeds.[2]

As a solution to the ills of his society, Voltaire proposed the elimination of the clergy from all political power and national independence from religion. He considered the clergy to be a particularly depraved lot, infected with avarice and hubris, aspiring only to extend their own dominion, and unworthy to rule over those impoverished by their greed. It is from avarice, not the love of truth and justice, that they promote the persecution of heretics and engender wars between nations. All the bloodshed in Europe is laid to their charge. The king is only a pawn in their hands. If the magistrate was left to his own secular devices and the clergy removed from his presence, he would rule with wisdom and justice, and peace would suffuse the land. The magistrate is not subject to the same depravity or avarice that religious leaders exude, although Voltaire never attempted to explain how this could be. He believed that despots are subject to enlightenment.[3]

In his later writings, when it was safer for him to reveal his true colors, Voltaire became a strident opponent of Christianity in general. Earlier, he could deny that he was a Christian and offer some muted criticisms of the religion, usually under the auspices of another man's opinion, but later he felt free to renounce the religion as a "virulent infection, terrifying madness, bloodthirsty monster." It was no longer the crimes of Christendom that he denounced with these words but the very essence of Christianity itself. It was not the Catholic Church but its sacred canon that led the religion down this path. The Old Testament is described as a compilation of monstrous stories about a sadistic God and a mingle-mangle of teachings that withstand all purity, charity, and reason. The New Testament is described as a mishmash of inept reason, outright lies, and contradictions "in almost every fact," and its stories are considered juvenile, superstitious, and fanatical. The cross itself stands for the assassination of rulers and the massacre of the innocent. Christianity must, therefore, be held in contempt. "Every sensible man, every honorable man, must hold Christianity in horror." His solution is to *écraser l'infâme* (crush the filth)—a phrase he repeats incessantly throughout his later works. The apparent meaning, although he is often guarded in its use, is to extirpate Christianity entirely. The self-professed man of tolerance is now prepared "to terminate and destroy the idol (i.e., Christianity) from top to bottom," and can even chide the rulers of the day for not acceding to his wishes.[4]

His own beliefs are most consonant with the *philosophies* of the Enlightenment: God is found in nature through reason, and good deeds are the true means of his service. This is all that he considers necessary for sound faith. Anything else is absurd. Miracle stories are ridiculous and theological disputes "the most terrible scourge of the world." Religion should be a simple matter of basic belief and good deeds without mixture of superstition or speculation. It represents the universal faith of humankind: belief in a Supreme Being—eternal, wise, and moral—whose general providence is beheld in the immutable laws of nature, and the exhortation to follow His laws in good, moral living.

> When reason, free from its shackles, will inform the people that there is only one God, that this God is the common Father of all men, who are brothers; that these men ought to be brothers one to another, good and just; that they ought to exercise all virtue; that God, being good and just, ought to reward these virtues and punish crimes: then, my brothers, men will be more disposed toward the good while less superstitious in nature.[5]

The spirit of Voltaire's deistic, anti-Christian philosophy was embodied across the sea within a number of the sons of liberty. This spirit has already been seen in the writings of Thomas Paine, the author of *Common Sense* and the *Age of Reason*, but it is necessary to illustrate its impact upon American culture once again through the patronage and influence of its greatest patriarch, Thomas Jefferson. While it is difficult to assess the direct influence that Voltaire exerted upon him, it is safe to say that Jefferson was a product of the same spirit, which permeated much of the age and much of his words. Jefferson was certainly not the creative genius of American mythology. Even he admitted in a letter to James Madison (30 August 1823) and Henry Lee (8 May 1825) that he was merely "a passive auditor of the opinions of others . . . neither aiming at originality of principle or sentiment," when he wrote the Declaration of Independence. John Adams considered the Declaration a compilation of the "hackneyed" phrases of the day, and it is hard to argue that this work or the rest of the Jeffersonian corpus can be interpreted in any other way.[6]

Like many of the sons of the Enlightenment, he believed that reason is "the empire of truth" and that it is able to establish the first principles of our existence, including the existence of God. The order, course, and intricate details of nature are said to provide clear testimony to a Supreme Being if we would only bother to employ our rational faculties and consider its design. He calls his beliefs at one point "rational Christianity" to emphasize the use of reason in arriving at his conclusions and to contrast his method with those who depend upon the revelation of God in Christ. But whatever the label, he is certainly not the typical Christian of his day, whom Jefferson despises as bigoted and idiotic. He rejects all talk of miracles in the Bible as contrary to the laws of nature, and he stridently repudiates the detailed doctrines of orthodox Christianity. His religion prefers to limit the conversation to a few, basic attributes of God and emphasizes the practical matters of ethical life over detailed metaphysical speculation. His religion does not depart in any essential way from what we have already witnessed in Voltaire.[7]

However, he does possess great admiration for Jesus of Nazareth. Jesus preached, in the estimation of Jefferson, the "most sublime morality which has ever fallen from the lips of man, . . . more pure and perfect than those of the most correct of the philosophers," especially in regard to its "universal philanthropy." His teaching was certainly a vast improvement upon Jewish ideas. Jefferson considered their concept of God to be sadistic and their ethics "repulsive & antisocial." While Jefferson does not accept all of Jesus' teaching (His spiritualism and forgiveness for repentant sinners are particularly rejected), he does consider himself a "real Christian," a follower of the true teachings of Jesus. These teachings stand in marked contrast not only to Judaism but to what is taught under the name of Christ in the church. That version of Christianity has completely corrupted what came from the historical Jesus through foreign, "platonizing" influences. Like many a liberal in the eighteenth and nineteenth centuries, he believed that the genuine precepts of Jesus are a diamond among the dunghill that the church has erected around His name. In the tradition of liberalism, he attempted to eliminate the corrupting influence of the church, which had already begun to exert itself in the writings of the New Testament, and cut and paste the Bible to create what is more suitable to his liking. *The Life and Morals of Jesus of Nazareth* (1820) represents his attempt to set forth that which speaks of his moral concerns—inner motives, love, charity, etc.—as the true teachings of the historical Jesus and discard from the account of the church whatever did not fit within this image.[8]

The church is accused of corrupting the moral teachings of Jesus through all the artificial constructions it created after His death. Jefferson considered the Apostle Paul to be "the first corruptor of the doctrines of Jesus," and the early church's belief in the miracles, deity, atonement, and resurrection of Christ an adulteration of His message. The later church only increased the perversion with its specialized dogmas concerning the Trinity, the sacramental presence of Christ, the hierarchy of the church, etc. He calls those who created such perversions "the real Antichrist."[9]

It is from his own religious convictions that Jefferson forged much of his political and social agenda. Religion is seen in his writings to have an important role in politics if it fits with his purpose and agrees with his general convictions. He was more than happy, for example, to speak of our political rights—liberty and equality—as if they were "unalienable rights" endowed by the God of nature and thus provided with ultimate justification. (He would certainly never submit these rights to social conditioning or the capricious acts of government.) No government can impose or dispose these rights. They are the eternal laws of God, provided in nature to all humankind, regardless of one's station in life or the decrees of human-made systems. Religion, morality, and politics are all one and the same.[10]

However, when he left his own religious and political agenda behind, he often wished to erect a wall between the two in order to eliminate his enemies. The man who would reduce religion to morality can now say that religion is a personal and private matter between our God and conscience and has nothing to do with our collective or political lives. In his most famous letter on the subject, written to the Danbury Baptist Association in Connecticut (1 January 1802), he interpreted the First Amendment to the Constitution as "building a wall of separation between church and state." The church and its clergy, whom he calls the true "enemies of liberty," must be removed from the government, and he often conducted vitriolic and Voltarian tirades to prove this point. These religious people are believed to have a special propensity toward bigotry and hatred that secular people like Jefferson do not have. The atrocities of humankind can be traced, almost exclusively, to their influence. During his presidency, Jefferson attempted to cleanse the government from religion—i.e., religion which he does not like. For example, he eliminated the national day of fasting and prayer—rituals that proponents of natural religion detest—overturning the precedent of his two predecessors, Washington and Adams. In his Second Inaugural Address, he said that the free exercise of religion "is placed by the constitution independent of the powers of the general government" as a justification for his decision.[11]

The duplicity of Thomas Jefferson in these and other matters has been a subject of much discussion in recent literature. While he is often portrayed in the hagiography of American history as a defender of religious tolerance and freedom of speech, a more sober account cannot affirm this portrait so simply. John Quincy Adams, after reading Jefferson's *Autobiography*, wondered whether the hero of the story had forgotten about his "double dealing character" and "deep duplicity." The man who had "sworn upon the altar of God, eternal hostility against every form of tyranny over the mind of man" was not always faithful to this oath. His words often exceeded his practice. Leonard Levy in his *Jefferson and Civil Liberties: The Darker Side* lists a number of hypocritical practices that marked Jefferson's career. He sought to prosecute Aaron Burr, based on mere rumor and suspicion after the courts had exonerated him; he supported a bill of attainder, which would convict a suspect without trial, against Josiah Philips, an alleged Tory outlaw; he rejected the Sedition Act, which required criminal intent and a jury trial in matters of libel; and he encouraged the prosecution of federalist papers for seditious libel against his republican government. These and other acts of hypocrisy are cited by Levy as evidence of Jefferson's darker side. In a stinging indictment Levy wrote that "Thomas Jefferson never once risked career or reputation to champion free speech, fair trial, or any other libertarian value." While these words sound harsh and need to be softened in a more balanced portrait, there still remains much room to criticize Jefferson's more typical, saintly image.[12] He is certainly not the Apostle Paul, a man who suffered much more hardship for the sake of his Gospel than Jefferson and the rest of his critics could ever imagine. Paul wrote,

> Five times I received from the Jews the forty lashes
> minus one . . . Three times I was beaten with rods,
> once I was stoned, three times I was shipwrecked, I
> spent a night and a day on the open sea. . . . I have
> labored and toiled and have often gone without sleep;
> I have known hunger and thirst and have often gone
> without food; I have been cold and naked. . . . I have
> worked much harder, been in prison more frequently,
> been flogged more severely, and been exposed to death
> again and again. (2 Cor. 11:23ff.)

Eventually he was beheaded.

Whether Jefferson should retain his exalted position among the pantheon of American gods is of no particular concern. There is no need to deprecate his character or discount what is truly worthy of emulation in the man. To judge his overall life or analyze his virtues and defects does not serve any purpose in the matter at hand. In fact, what is of utmost concern is a matter for which he often receives high marks, even among his most severe critics, and the matter is only of concern because of its lasting impact on American society and the abject hypocrisy of those who continue to espouse it.

The matter of particular concern is public education. Most scholars and educators hail Jefferson as the father of secular, public education in this country. Jefferson envisaged an America in which education would be provided at the public expense. Every child would be taught basic skills in reading, writing, and arithmetic, and certain students would be afforded the opportunity for more advanced learning at higher levels. This education would be secular in nature, by which he meant to exorcise all Christian ministers, readings, ideas, and exercises from the classroom and school board. He would then substitute under the banner of secularity his own array of teachers, courses, and ideas.[13] Secular scholars have praised this concept and rightfully so. It has provided them with free money to propagate their ideas and a public platform on which to do so.

But it contains a big lie—the lie of neutral, secular education—and Jefferson knew it. The man who crusaded against the church receiving public money, contending that it is unconscionable "to compel a man to furnish contributions of money for the propagation of opinions which he disbelieves," really wants tax payers to propagate Jeffersonian dogma when all is said and done. This is his design. This is the real agenda. Of course, he can spout the typical, liberal tripe about "neutrality" in public education, but this is merely a bill of goods sold for the consumption of an unsuspecting public. There is no such commodity for sale. This is only a facade that secular people like Jefferson erect in order to shove their religious dogma down everyone's throat and exclude their opponents from participation in the process.

Let us take for example the University of Virginia. Thomas Jefferson was the founder, rector, and architect of the school. It was established in January 1819 by an act of the Virginia legislature in accordance with the designs of Jefferson and its commissioners. These designs did not call for unbiased academic freedom or pluralism and are clearly marked by Jefferson's own religious and political agenda. This can be seen in a number of areas. One, Jefferson's disdain for Christianity is marked by his elimination of all professors of divinity from the school. This same move he had proposed earlier in regard to William and Mary, and while unsuccessful in the legislature, he finally enacted it on his own as a visitor to the college. This same proposal was now to mark his own university. The various sects of the Christian church were told that they must educate their members with their own hands and leave the premises of the university. When cries of atheism rang out against Jefferson over this proposal, he grudgingly permitted the Christians to establish schools around the university, although not upon its official grounds. They could minister to students who sought them out, but they must remain off campus and separate from the real power-base of the university—separate and unequal. Two, Jefferson in the true spirit of liberalism placed his own religion within the curriculum but put it surreptitiously under a different name, hoping to disguise his true intentions. He proposed that the professor of ethics should instruct the students in natural religion—"the proofs of the being of God, the creator, preserver, and supreme ruler of the universe, the author of all the relations of morality, and of the laws and obligations these infer. . . ."—all the religious principles that Jefferson found necessary to believe. It would just not be called religion. It would go by a different name, so that no one would notice. The same religious principles, in fact, could be protected in the rest of the curriculum through the same name game. Third, the political purpose for the school was to propagate Jefferson's republican agenda. He felt that federalist ideas were taking over the north, and he hoped to inculcate republicanism, particularly in the law school, and stack the legislatures of the country with his clones. Professors were to fit Jefferson's political persuasions, and materials must be approved by the board in accordance with this standard. Jefferson, for example, wanted the "tory" (federalist) ideas in David Hume's *The History of England* doctored and recommended that an abridged, "republicanized" version of the work be used instead.[14]

It is out of Jefferson's own political and religious designs that he supports the separation of church and state. The doctrine is ostensibly proposed to promote religious freedom and might have done so in certain areas; however, the real agenda for Jefferson is not the freedom of religion but the freedom from religion—i.e., the Christian religion—in the public sphere. His animus toward Christianity is well documented. His particular concerns about its relationship to the public sector contain all the typical prejudices of the day. The church is charged with fostering bigotry through its dogmatic pronouncements and is held accountable for most of the atrocities that have transpired since the beginning of civilization.

The most eloquent response to the charges of Jefferson and the other cultured despisers of the day was provided by the German theologian, Friedrich Schleiermacher. His great work, *On Religion: Speeches to its Cultured Despisers*, first appeared in the summer of 1799 when he was working as an unknown chaplain in a Berlin hospital. It became an immediate success, and Schleiermacher went on to become one of the great theologians of modern times. His work *On Religion* provides an answer to those who would ridicule the church as bigoted and antiquated. He defended the church by maintaining that the true source of religion, the feelings or passions of the human soul, can never be adequately expressed by anyone in this world, whether through word or deed, and this includes both the church as well as the sons of the Enlightenment. All of us fall short of the divine glory. He thought it incredibly shortsighted to reject the church because of the cold shell of orthodoxy or its dogmatic scholasticism. It is the kernel, not the overt form or husk, that bears witness to what is ultimate, and to criticize its confession as inadequate or fallible is only to state what is obvious. No one can truly speak of a God who transcends our experience or declare His will with absolute certitude. What is true of our words is even more the case in regard to our deeds. Even the best of them when placed under the microscope of divine righteousness fall short of the divine image. Of course, Christians are hypocrites, but so is Jefferson. Of course, Puritans conduct witch-hunts, but so does Jefferson. To read history in a selective manner, highlighting the dark pages of the church's past and extolling secular regimes as free from sin, is the worst sort of revisionism. Can one say that Kubla and Genghis Kahn were less depraved than medieval Christendom or preferable to its not-so-infallible Popes? Can one say that the French Revolution and its guillotine were qualitatively better than Papal inquisitions, or Robespierre than Pope Pius VI? Even if one would make this case in Schleiermacher's day, certainly those who have lived through the secular atrocities of the twentieth century—Nazism and Communism—cannot believe that atheistic regimes deliver on their promises to create a millennial kingdom in the here and now. In fact, it would seem quite the contrary. The most secular states of the twentieth century have been indicted time and again for committing the most vile transgressions against fundamental, human rights.

The doctrine of church/state separation is often thought to be embodied in the First Amendment to the Constitution, but this interpretation goes far beyond what is present in the text. Certainly, if Jefferson and Madison had obtained their ultimate designs, the amendment would have called for a complete separation of church and state, but the amendment does not state this in any clear way. Even Madison, the original draftsman of the amendment, appeared to interpret its words in a narrow sense as merely prohibiting the establishment of "a national religion." At least those are his comments as recorded in the annals of Congress (5 August 1789). There is no talk of a separation between the sacred and the secular. There is only the desire to prevent the American government from following the example of Europe and establishing a religious institution of its own. While the states are free to continue their practice— many of which allowed townships to establish a church in their district, the federal government would not seek to establish such an institution; and that is all. Nothing else is spelled out. The final form of the amendment reads: "Congress shall make no law respecting an establishment of religion, or prohibiting the free exercise thereof." If more is intended by these words (and the words are ambiguous), there is little direct proof of this in the debates over its language. The few comments that remain from the states during the ratification process do not indicate much, and if anything, lean toward the narrow reading of the text. In the State of Virginia, for example, the Anti-Federalists are seen to follow this reading and reject the amendment accordingly, as *not* calling for the separation of church and state.

The 3d amendment [the First Amendment], recommended by Congress, does not prohibit the rights of
conscience from being violated or infringed; and although it goes to restrain Congress from passing
laws establishing any national religion, they might,
notwithstanding, levy taxes to any amount, for the
support of religion or its preachers; and any particular denomination of Christians might be so favored
and supported by the General Government, as to
give it a decided advantage over others, and in process of time render it as powerful and dangerous as
if it was established as the national religion of the
country.[15]

Whatever one's reading of the original intention, it must
also be said that its provisions still need to be translated into
the modern era. Any literal force that it possesses is still
subject to the changing conditions of the nation. Certainly,
after the Civil War, the entire Bill of Rights lost much of
the original power that it possessed to protect the states
against federal invasion. The Fourteenth Amendment was
enacted at that time to protect all U.S. citizens against the
states and became the means by which the federal courts
abrogated its own amendments and the powers it had given
to the states. Henceforth, a literal reading of its amendments could only be considered mythology. The nation had
moved on and the issues had moved on as well. Whatever
was intended in the past only became a means that was
either deconstructed or simply manipulated to fit the standards of an ever-evolving nation.[16]

In the twentieth century, the Supreme Court decided to
erect Jefferson's wall between church and state and manipulated the Constitution accordingly. Armed with an expanding federal government and a growing secular culture, the
Court attempted to eliminate religion from the public arena
and relegate its influence to the bottom and edges of society.
Justice Hugo Black started the ball rolling in *Everson v.
Board of Education* (1947) when he announced that the First

Amendment of the Constitution "has erected a wall between church and state," which is "high and impregnable." In writing for the majority, he cited the authority of Jefferson and Madison to prove that the Court's interpretation is historically based and then repeated all the typical prejudices that his patriarchs wielded against religious people in order to demonstrate the necessity for building a wall. These people are held responsible for most of the "turmoil, civil strife, and persecutions" of the past in their attempts to wield power. It is, therefore, necessary to keep them from the centers of power and in this case to keep tax dollars out of their pockets. "No tax in any amount, large or small, can be levied to support any religious activities or institutions, whatever they may be called, or whatever form they may adopt to teach or practice religion."[17]

The next year the Court carried out its intentions with legalistic precision as it declared unconstitutional voluntary religious instruction within the public schools. A local school board in Champaign, Illinois had provided space during regular school hours for students to receive religious instruction in the faith of their choice. Students could opt out of this instruction if their parents did not wish them to participate, but these students would need to attend secular classes during that period. In spite of the voluntary nature of the program, the Court struck it down in the name of its wall. It maintained that both church and state "best work to achieve their lofty aims if each is left free from the other within its respective spheres." While it denied that its intentions were hostile to religion, its comments about "lofty aims" appear to be patronizing and the effect of the ruling clearly reduces religion to a secondary role in society, if not total irrelevancy in our collective lives.[18]

In numerous cases thereafter, the Court attempted to sort religion out of a society that had been steeped in its traditions for centuries, but the decisions lacked consistency. Sometimes it favored the continued practice (military chaplains, congressional prayers, manger scenes, etc.), using the most elliptical forms of justification, and other times it discontinued certain practices (school prayer, Bible reading, posting of the Ten Commandments, etc.), maintaining its wall. The inconsistency of its position so bothered the Court that by 1971 their "wall" had become more like a "line," and that line was considered to be "a blurred, indistinct, and variable barrier." And yet, the justices still persisted in the notion that society should be "secular" and religion should be a "private matter." In *Lemon v. Kurtzman* (1971) they tried to develop three tests to determine whether a statute would pass constitutional muster:

> Every analysis in this area must begin with consideration of the cumulative criteria developed by the Court over many years. Three such tests may be gleaned from our cases. First, the statute must have a secular legislative purpose; second, its principal or primary effect must be one that neither advances nor inhibits religion, . . . ; finally, the statute must not foster "an excessive government entanglement with religion." (Walz, supra, at 674, 25 L.Ed.2d at 704)

These criteria have proved to be helpful to the Court in deciding subsequent cases.[19]

The criteria have proved to be so helpful to the Court's understanding that it is necessary to respond to each one of them separately. The proposal is to display some of the difficulties with the criteria below and then provide a fuller exposition of these comments in the rest of the chapter.

The first criterion is considered problematic because it assumes without warrant or justification that the legislature could simply detach itself from religion and enact laws that are purely secular in nature. The problem with this position is that all laws speak of one's vision in life (*Weltanschauung*), one's moral ideals, and one's divine standards. While a state might profess to be secular or godless, it only belies the true nature of its being; for without God there would be no purpose or ideal standard from which to justify any of its agenda or even proceed with legislation. A secular world could never provide the impetus to transcend what it *is* and become what it *ought* to be. It contains no ideal vantage point from which to create a better world or aspire to that which is higher and beyond. The legislature and the Court can only pretend that it is secular by playing the name game and denying the true nature of what they do. They can only call what they do secular and what their opponents do religious. Take, for example, the Court's decision in *Stone v. Graham* (1980). The Court decided in this case that it was unconstitutional to post the Ten Commandments in a classroom because the text in which these commands are found is associated with the Judeo-Christian tradition and the worship of God is specifically mentioned in the first table. The text is, therefore, considered sacred by the Court and must be censored accordingly.[20] But what is considered sacred to the Court can suddenly become "secular" when it relates to its own civil religion. The Declaration of Independence is a good case in point, where a sacred text becomes secular, when it works to the Court's advantage. Even though it speaks directly of "nature's God" and the inalienable rights with which He has endowed us, it is protected as a secular document by the Court and can be displayed proudly and inculcated zealously with all its moral ideals throughout our public institutions. The reason can only reside in the power of the Court to apply the name game, however it wants and wherever it wants and whenever it wants to suit its purpose. What is sacred to the Court can become secular to the Court when it is useful in the propagation of its dogma. All that is needed is the will to power.

The second criterion we find problematic because it pretends that legislation can somehow be neutral in nature, neither advancing nor inhibiting religion. One would think that the myth of neutrality had been put to rest centuries ago when philosophers recognized that our own subjectivity permeated all things; and if that was not sufficient, one would wonder how anyone could continue to speak this way in the postmodern world where all our concepts and actions are said to be filled with social and cultural bias. But the Supreme Court seems to live in the eighteenth century where rational objectivity and neutrality were still conceivable. They seem to think that one could provide tax dollars to those who are secular and ask them to be neutral about religion and its ideas, as if they have no specific agenda of their own in this regard. The Court does not seem to even notice the antagonistic, left-wing bias of education today, which such policies have created, and the flight of religious people into their own private schools. The Court seems only concerned about bias when traditional, religious ideas cause humiliation and embarrassment to those who disagree with them,[21] but seems to care little when the patrons of these religions experience the same type of offense at the hands of feminists, Freudians, Darwinians, postmodernists, et al. and are forced to leave the school system.[22] The schools, of course, cannot help but advance a position and inhibit others if their teaching is to have substance, but to pretend that their agenda is neutral or objective is nothing but pure hypocrisy and defies all that we learn in education today. The Supreme Court should know better than this and stop pretending that schools, the courts, or the government in general does not advance or inhibit certain religious forms. The Supreme Court, as the moral conscience of the nation, does nothing but advance religion—its own religion—and should stop pretending that it can do otherwise.

The third criterion prohibits a statute that is enacted by the legislature from fostering an "excessive government entanglement with religion." It incurs many of the criticisms that have already been related in the discussion of the first two criteria concerning the religious nature of government and the impossibility of neutral policies, and they need not be reiterated here. The only matter that needs to be added to this analysis concerns the heritage of the country and its ongoing influence in our lives. From this historical perspective, it is difficult to understand how the Supreme Court could possibly disentangle a government that was conceived by Christian people and informed by Christian ideas from its origin, especially since its founding documents and concepts have not essentially changed from its conception. Much of the basic outline of our government contains notions that were fostered in its Puritan heritage—democracy, equality, capitalism, etc.—and filled with religious principles—inalienable rights, natural law, moral ideals, etc.—from Christian and non-Christian sources. How is it possible for the Supreme Court to exorcise religion from the country when its own Constitution was conceived in this womb and dedicated to these ideas? The answer can only lie in the constant drumbeat of those who identify themselves with secularity, pretend that their ideas or lineage are otherwise, and hope to exorcise this aspect of our heritage from America today. There is certainly no philosophical or historical reason for doing so, and it would appear that pure, secular prejudice is its primary motive. It is certainly not the love for dispassionate, objective analysis that causes the Court to select the most secular fathers of the past (e.g., Jefferson and Madison) and their most secular words in its cases and ignore all else. The Court simply prefers to deny, negate, and ignore when faced with the historical and philosophical basis of its principles and practice the worst sort of revisionism—all in the pretense of separating church and state, all in the hope of disentangling the government from religion, and all for the sake of a notion that is ridiculous and impossible from the very outset. There is no way to separate church and state, beyond the philosophical naïveté, historical revisionism, and secular prejudice of the Court.

What the government promotes in the public arena is never free from religious ramifications. In fact, the government, far from being neutral in matters of religion, promulgates its civil religion with utmost zeal and piety through numerous standards, memorials, and rites. The flag, the Washington Mall, the Fourth of July, and the Pledge of Allegiance are all designed to promote devotion to the country and dedication to its principles among the citizens of the

land. Public schools are devoted to spread the dogma of the
state through the various subjects, texts, and teachers that it
specifies and sanctions. The Supreme Court says that "teachers shall be of good moral character and patriotic disposition, that certain studies plainly essential to good citizenship
must be taught, and that nothing be taught which is mani-
festly inimical to the public welfare."[23]

There are many groups through the ages who have re-
sisted the civil religion of a country, considering it a form of
idolatry or nationalistic bigotry. The early Christians would
not take an unconditional oath to Caesar or participate in
the cult of the emperor because they felt that this *sacramen-
tum* (oath/mystery) conflicted with their own unconditional
obligation to serve God and serve Him only. They refused
to participate in many aspects of their society due to this
conflict. The Confessional Church of Hitler's Germany
would not recognize any other source of their theology than
Jesus Christ, as they fought long and hard against the "German Christian" mentality to identify Germanism or National Socialism with Christianity. Karl Barth, one of its
leading theologians, called Nazism an "anti-Christian counter
church" and refused to take an oath of allegiance to Hitler,
preferring instead to flee to Switzerland.

In this country, there are a number of groups who could
be mentioned as antagonists of the civil religion. Probably
the most infamous in the eyes of the American public are
the Jehovah's Witnesses, who refuse to salute the flag, serve
in the military, and participate in the political process. But
regardless of the group, none of them feels that this country
is worthy of his or her devotion, and all of them are deeply
offended by the civil religion. This offense, of course, works
both ways. The average American, whose sense of duty
includes both God and country, is deeply offended by these
groups, often calling them "unpatriotic" or "un-American,"
and the dissidents who prefer to remain separate from this
consortium can spew forth their own repertoire of invectives
in turn. The offense is indeed unfortunate and can be miti-

gated whenever possible, but it can never be totally eliminated. It is unavoidable whenever matters of serious mo-
ment confront us in national policy and the government
must reject neutrality in order to take a stand. Even if the
majority might come along with that stand and come along
without offense, someone will necessarily be offended.

Secular culture cannot create a world that is free from
meaning and religious significance. Even its most concerted
efforts of late to create inclusive symbols and holidays will
always remain offensive to certain segments of society. Neutral symbols and celebrations do not exist. The government,
for example, in its attempt to denude Christmas, Easter,
and Thanksgiving of their specific Christian content through
the use of "neutral" symbols cannot cease to represent
someone's belief, however it chooses to celebrate. Multicultural symbols do not represent everybody, only multicultural
religion. Secular symbols represent a nation that has shunned
its Christian heritage and no longer wishes to find God in
its cultic expressions. In fact, nothing has become more
offensive to Christian sensibilities than the secular and
material view of its sacred days represented by the culture at
large.

In the twentieth century, the theory of evolution has
become one of the most talked-about areas of offense among
religious people in our country. It is this particular matter of
offense that has brought the issue of church/state separation
to the forefront and must receive special attention in any
discussion of the issue. The theory is sure to cause continual
controversy in our society since the vast majority of Americans believe that God created human beings; some believing
that he used direct means in accordance with the book of
Genesis (44 percent) and others a more indirect approach as
if guiding a process (38 percent). The theory is a decided
attack upon the former group as it negates a literal interpretation of their sacred book; and against the latter it can
become offensive depending upon the form in which the
theory is presented. Sometimes the rancor of the evolution-
ists can become direct and intense.

Richard Dawkins has written that anyone who denies evolution is either "ignorant, stupid or insane (or wicked—but I'd rather not consider that.)" It isn't a big step from calling someone wicked to taking forceful measures to put an end to their wickedness. John Maddox, the editor of *Nature*, has written in his journal that "it may not be long before the practice of religion must be regarded as anti-science." In his recent book *Darwin's Dangerous Idea*, philosopher Daniel Dennett compares religious believers—90 percent of the population—to wild animals who may have to be caged, and he says that parents should be prevented (presumably by coercion) from misinforming their children about the truth of evolution, which is so evident to him.[24]

The offense has involved the courts in a number of cases, but the most famous occurred in Dayton, Tennessee during the summer of 1925. Several southern states had passed anti-evolutionary legislation during the spring of that year. John Scopes, a high school coach and science teacher, tested the law in both the classroom and the courtroom but was found guilty in accordance with that law. However, outside the Bible Belt, in the north among the presses and the universities, where the theory had dominated for years, the south was convicted of abject stupidity, along with all its chicken coops, backward yokels, and fundamentalist beliefs. Clarence Darrow, the lawyer for the defense, was portrayed as a sophisticated, urban agnostic, who was leading the crusade against "bigots and ignoramuses" controlling the school system. His rival in the courtroom was William Jennings Bryan, a former presidential candidate. Bryan was depicted as a dim-witted fool, "the idol of Morondum" according to Darrow, for his patronage of the fundamentalist cause and his foolhardy defense of the Scripture when he took the stand in the midst of the trial. The ridicule of the fundamentalist intellect and conservative religion in general was unrelenting after the case and has become a staple among the intellectual elite of this country ever since.

The literal interpretation of the Bible, which is so often identified with Fundamentalism, was actually the aftermath of the Protestant Reformation and the legacy of all Protestantism in general at the beginning of this century. The Reformation emphasized literal interpretation because of the many abuses that allegorical methods had brought to the text in the Middle Ages. It simply reacted to the other side of the debate and took everything in Scripture, including the six days of creation, in a literal manner. In the Middle Ages, the account of Genesis was seldom understood in this way. Gregory the Great believed that God created all things as "seeds" and brought forth their potency afterwards in successive periods of time. Thomas Aquinas said that the days in Genesis one "denote merely sequence in the natural order, as Augustine holds (*Gen. ad lit.* iv, 34) and not succession in time ... or ordinary days measured by a solar circuit." Evolutionary theory, which extended back to pre-Socratic days, was considered compatible with this interpretation.

> Since the generation of one thing is the corruption of another, it was not inconsistent with the original forming of things for the higher to be brought forth out of the corruption of the lower. Hence animals that are generated from the corruption of inanimate objects, or of plants, could have been generated then. Those that are generated out of the corruption of animals, however, could not have been produced then, except incipiently.[25]

The Reformation, however, would have none of this and preferred a simpler reading of the text. This method of interpretation would dominate the reading of all texts in the western world for the next few centuries. Even liberalism when it arrived in full force during the nineteenth century did not reinterpret those parts of Scripture that it found offensive—the six days of creation, the Garden of Eden, the miracle accounts, etc.—but preferred to interpret them literally or historically and reject them accordingly from their system of belief. It has not been until recent times that Protestants have begun to rethink their approach to the text. Rudolf Bultmann's program of demythologizing, Hans Frei's narrative theology, and Jacques Derrida's deconstructionism, which now permeates all the humanities, are just a few examples that can be cited of more recent approaches.

Even a conservative like Karl Barth no longer interpreted the text in a simple, literal manner but preferred to interpret its message through the in-between concept of saga—"an intuitive and poetic picture of a pre-historical reality of history which is enacted once and for all within the confines of time and space." His interpretation of Genesis one provides a good case in point. In it, he emphasizes the ineffable character of origins, as God's creative activity is brought forth in a prosodical and transcendent manner, and questions concerning metaphysical realities and the true nature of creation are more in view than the petty concerns of history and science. After the title of the chapter in verse one, verse two is said to begin the history of God's creative activity. God's work is meant to contrapose the formless void (*tohu wabohu*), the chaotic waters (*mayim*), and the darkness of the abyss (*choshek*, *tehom*), which are encountered in the verse. Such a state can in no way be attributed to the work of God but refers instead in the Hebrew language to the inimical forces of a most sinister, negating evil in which God will bring forth what is good—in the darkness, He will bring forth light; in the void, He will establish His order (*raquia*); in the waters, He will bring forth life; and in the chaos, He will create His days and weeks and years. The darkness is said to be separated, and the waters bounded (Jer. 5:22). Later, in the world to come, these forces of vanity will be driven from the new heaven and new earth and will be no more (Rev. 21:1, 3). The false lights (Satan and his angels) will be sentenced to their darkness, even the temporal lights (the sun, the moon, and the stars) will lose their luster (Matt. 24:29, Isa. 60:19). The true Sun of Righteousness, the only Morning Star (Jesus), will outshine all pretenders and illuminate His subjects with the light of His presence "all in all" (Mal. 4:2, Rev. 22:5, 16, 1 Cor. 15:28). The end will only consummate what took place in the beginning. The interpretation of Genesis one finds its fulfillment in Revelation 22, where the metaphysical forces of darkness are defeated and the victory is won. These metaphysical forces subsume the literal plane of space and time and become the focus of the entire Scripture. The petty concerns of science are not even in view.[26]

No matter how one wishes to interpret the passage, literally or figuratively, it can never be reconciled in its entirety with the atheistic implications of Darwin's concepts. Evolutionary theory can speak of God if it views life in an Aristotelian manner as moving toward more complex and sublime forms, and the Scripture might find reconciliation with this interpretation of the theory, but not with Darwin's. Darwin believed that evolutionary change does not imply improvement or progress as if life were moving toward some ultimate goal. Change is simply change, and what evolves has much to do with the happenstance of life. No design or God is necessary to explain it. The reason that plants gravitate toward the sun has nothing to do with the purpose for which they were made or some appointed end to which they were designed but the simple fact that those which did not do so are no longer around, and that is all. To introduce God or design into the equation is simply unnecessary because life can be explained without this postulate. God is not needed to explain how life evolved when mechanisms like the survival of the fittest can do just as well without Him.

Whether in its Darwinian or non-Darwinian form, the theory of evolution offends many religious people, and this offense cannot be avoided. Theories do have implications, and serious theories have serious implications for our overall view of life. One should not ignore those implications or pretend that they do not exist. One should not relegate speech to trivial matters to avoid conflict or prevent others from speaking when it conflicts with one's way of thinking. Clarence Darrow complained in the midst of the Scopes' trial that Jennings wanted to stop "every man of science and learning in the world because he does not believe in your fool religion;" and his comment should be heeded, despite its imprecatory tone. Our speech should not be silenced by religious dogma nor relegated to innocuous matters that are irrelevant to its questions, no matter how great the offense. Free speech that does not offend someone is also not worth uttering. But the freedom to offend must work both ways. If our schools are free to attack religion, then they must also be free to defend it. Those who protect the rights of a school to attack religion cannot argue that religious ideas must be silenced because some might disagree. This argument can only be offered out of pure hypocrisy and probably harbors a special contempt for certain religious groups, which it finds offensive and does not mind offending.

The Supreme Court still remains hostile to theories identified with religious motives. In *Edward v. Aguillard* (1987) the Court decided that creation science could not demand a place alongside the theory of evolution, even if it was put forth in an attempt to balance the curriculum. The State of Louisiana had passed legislation requiring the teaching of creation science whenever and wherever the theory of evolution was taught, but the Court found that this so-called "balanced treatment" bill was unduly prejudicial to the theory of evolution. It felt that schoolteachers already possessed the flexibility to supplant theories of origin with current science, whenever and wherever it might lead them; although in concurring opinions, several justices joined in rejecting creation science altogether as a genuine alternative to the theory of evolution, since the motives behind its propagation were seen as religious. While one can study religion in an objective, nonpartisan manner, these jurists felt that one is not allowed to advance it in the classroom. Only secular and anti-religious ideas are given this special protection, and only they can be advanced in the classroom as worthy of belief.[27]

This oppression is most significant because unlike other matters involving church/state relations the elimination of the church and its ideals from education touches the soul of American democracy. In a democracy, the education of the public is most essential to the nation because the people rule the country and must rule wisely. "In [democracy] alone the government is entrusted to each citizen. . . . Therefore, in a republic, everything depends upon establishing this love, and education should attend to inspiring it."[28]

The Court's decisions have helped to facilitate the anti-religious atmosphere that is so prevalent on our campuses today and destroy the souls of our children.[29] This anti-religious bias must become the main focus of any discussion of church/state relations—all else is secondary when it comes to the matter of education. The bias comes under many different names—multiculturalism, postmodernism, deconstructionism, etc.—which often feign inclusiveness, but they all represent the same anti-religious dogma in the end. All of them preach that values are relative to one's cultural background, and all of them renounce the quest for any transcendent or absolute truth which would provide guidance in life or present a means of settling our differences.

This position, of course, is not new. It has a long history within western culture, beginning with the Sophists and receiving its latest impulse from the writings of Nietzsche, Heidegger, and Dewey. The problem that arises in our country certainly should not discredit this tradition as if it has nothing to say or contribute to the ongoing debate. Cultural bias does color much of what we say, and there is no way to enrapture ourselves above the time and space in which we live. Our sex, race, culture, and background permeate all that we say and do, and it is arrogant to believe that one can speak or act as a god and transcend the conditions of one's birth. In fact, the Supreme Court could learn much from this postmodern perspective in its pretense of neutral and nonpartisan policies toward religion.

The problem that arises in our country has more to do with the absence of any forces to balance the excesses of this position than the falsehood of its suppositions. The American representatives of the movement, unlike their European counterparts, lack balance and nuance in their treatment, and since they have few to rival them, they often become more of a caricature of a viewpoint than what would otherwise be demanded in the academic community.

To illustrate our concerns, let us consider two of the most celebrated humanities' professors in this country—Richard Rorty and Stanley Fish—and their postmodern analysis. These men are all-too-representative of the anti-religious bias in education today. Their position is advanced with much zeal as the current rage of academia and the funding to proselyte and indoctrinate their cause comes to a large extent from the coffers of the state or at least under the guise of pluralism.

Richard Rorty is a professor of Humanities at the University of Virginia. He believes like many linguists today that it is impossible to free ourselves from our culture and establish the veracity of what we say and do. There is no foundation to our knowledge, no source to justify what we believe as a culture, no higher criteria to judge the claims of any discipline, and no means to adjudicate between competing theories of science, mathematics, religion, or philosophy. We cannot settle our differences or establish any viewpoint whatsoever. When we talk we are simply "saying something—participating in a conversation rather than contributing to an inquiry." Our conversation is a social game with which we indulge ourselves as blue collar workers or highbrow scholars, but none of it, no matter what the level, can settle anything among ourselves or judge others who subsist outside its rules. All of it amounts to a semantic game, and all of it is subject to interpretation, whose form is pure rhetoric, whose content is pure sophistry, and whose substance is pure bullshit.[30]

Rorty rejects all claims to establish objective criteria, whether it comes from the positivists' trust in nature or the idealists' belief in divine realities. The sentences that we utter are only sentences, connected with other sentences and producing their own inner reality, but are incapable of raising the question of meaning or reference. They do not provide a mirror-image of nature as if corresponding to external reality or making contact with the real world. They do not raise the specter of truth and goodness as if expressing some metaphysical or divine reality. They are simply enclosed within themselves and contain no reference to God or this world. They cannot even discriminate between theories and judge what is better—fascism or capitalism, Ptolemy or Copernicus, truth or falsehood, love or hate. All is subject to conventional biases, and no ultimate standard is available to judge what is better or worse, what is right or wrong. Sentences only refer to themselves, and outside their own reality all else is dead, physics and metaphysics alike.[31]

Stanley Fish, a professor at Duke University, is also a noted spokesman of this point of view. He joins Rorty and the rest of the postmodern world in the all-too-familiar harangue against universals, absolutes, values, and reason. Life, he says, does not contain these "higher or more general constraints," only different constraints, which are engendered in local contexts and manufactured by varied interests and agendas. Our values, reasons, and criteria are the product of a historically conditioned consciousness, which cannot be examined or scrutinized or evaluated by that which transcends it. It would only be possible to examine our beliefs or make progress toward some goal if we existed as "contextual and unsituated" entities and were in contact with universal, abstract truth. But we have no such vantage point, no sense of what is right or wrong, beyond our own limited and totally biased perspectives. All that we say and do is relative to a certain perspective in life, and this perspective can in no way address the human race as if it were universal, absolute, moral, or rational. "[Y]ou can never get away from your beliefs, which means that you can never get away from force, from the pressure exerted by a partial, non-neutral, nonauthoritative, ungrounded point of view."[32]

This means that all perspectives are equally one-sided, and all agendas reflect nothing beyond the exercise of power to enhance the interests of some group. Even feminists who complain about this patriarchal society only wish to remove the dominion of white males and replace it with their own. No one speaks from a neutral or objective point of view, or promotes fairness and equity in the market place. All our social and moral consciousness arise from our situation in life (*Sitz im Leben*) and the conventional ideas associated with that context, and none of us can speak outside of its rules and reasons and perspectives. Our condition does not permit us to speak for the human race in general, and we have no Word from God to declare what His will might be. We cannot even justify what we are to do with our own space, let alone speak for all people in all circumstances and at all times. And so, Fish can exhort us to exercise our bias and exalt in our provincial ideas, because prejudice and bigotry are the only conditions of life.

> The moral is clear and it is my moral: bias is just another word for seeing from a particular perspective as opposed to seeing from no perspective at all, and since seeing from no perspective at all is not a possibility, bias is a condition of consciousness and therefore of action.[33]

Of course, there are some voices in the academic community that oppose the excesses of the postmodern world, especially in regard to its war against the *logos* (reason). Most of them attempt to display what we as rational beings have in common. Noam Chomsky believes that language arises from a common, "biological endowment" and has constructed a universal grammar to demonstrate this; Claude Lévi-Strauss believes that all cultures function in accordance with certain structural laws and provides anthropological studies to demonstrate this; Hans-Georg Gadamer believes that the whole human race participates in a universal experience and shared tradition; Jürgen Habermas believes that we all possess a rational and universal capacity to communicate with each other and reach agreement in society. But most of the voices that challenge postmodernism come from overseas, and the few that arise in America find reservations only in a left-wing political agenda, which cannot be totally reconciled with its tenets. It is all-too-typical in the United States to find scholars who extol the virtues of postmodernism—only to emasculate its more disturbing implications, do an about-face, and continue to promote a rainbow coalition of left-wing causes. The one voice that represents the most decided and consistent protest against the postmodern world is silenced by the courts and the politically correct from participating in the process.

It is this voice that presents the ultimate ground for opposition, as it is this voice that postmodernism opposes most vehemently. The opposition reaches back to its patriarch, Friedrich Nietzsche, for its anti-Christian agenda. It was Nietzsche who set the agenda for postmodernism and set its sights directly against the Christian faith. Nietzsche believed that Christianity was an illness and its practitioners belonged in a lunatic asylum. It is these weak and sickly people who invented God to soothe their own unhappiness, and it is time that we become emancipated from this dependency and grow up. He condemns Christianity "with the most terrible accusation that an accuser has ever had in his mouth. To my mind, it is the greatest of all conceivable corruptions . . . the one great curse, the one enormous and innermost perversion." He hopes to deconstruct all dependence upon its metaphysics as the religion of the weak and inspire us to become more self-reliant. What he wants are creators, lawgivers, supermen, who will create their own meaning and values and no longer look to the heavens for a moral compass or a rational answer to life's problems.[34]

But without direction, Nietzsche had difficulty in providing a more positive vision for our lives, and he only

seemed to find definition in his nihilistic deconstruction of
Christian metaphysics. He had difficulty in defining himself
as anything other than a non-Christian; and so he lives only
as an antithesis to the more positive thesis of Christ; as an
atheist, not a theist; as an Antichrist, not a second Christ.
He lives by attacking Christian theism, and yet without it,
he would have nothing to oppose and nothing to say. In his
later work, *The Antichrist*, he stated this most directly:

> That which a theologian considers true, *must* of ne-
> cessity be false: this furnishes almost the criterion of
> truth. It is his most profound self-preservative in-
> stinct which forbids reality ever to attain to honour
> in any way, or even to raise its voice. Whithersoever
> the influence of the theologian extends, *valuations*
> are topsy-turvy, and the concepts "true" and "false"
> have necessarily changed places: that which is most
> deleterious to life, is here called "true," that which
> enhances it, elevates it, says Yea to it, justifies it and
> renders it triumphant, is called "false." . . . The Chris-
> tian Church allowed nothing to escape from its cor-
> ruption; it converted every value into its opposite,
> every truth into a lie, and every honest impulse into
> an ignominy of the soul.[35]

Nietzsche sets the agenda for the postmodern world by re-
nouncing those who follow the church and by defining his
own beliefs in terms of this negation.

In America, his disciples did much the same, but the
difference is that they had few to oppose them. (At least in
Basel, where Nietzsche taught for so many years, there were
other intellectuals like Karl Barth to balance the excesses of
his program.) In America, the voice of the church has been
so muted by federal policies and opposing forces that the
voice of postmodernism reigns practically unmolested. The
atmosphere that has been set by the Court and its wall has
helped to facilitate the ascendency of left-wing, anti-religious sentiment on our college campuses, and its opponents
are no longer heard. While the Court claims that it is against

hostility to religion, it has certainly helped to create a public platform for those who have a decided prejudice against traditional, religious views. The Court needs only to look outside the window and see what has transpired in our society *de facto*. Public education has become an enemy of religion in general and conservative, religious people in particular.

Notes

1. P. Gay, *Voltaire's Politics: The Poet as Realist* (New York: Vintage Books, 1965), 234-235, 243; D. Mornet, *Les Origines Intellectuelles de la Révolution Française 1715-1787* (Paris: Librairie Armand Colin, 1967), 226.

2. *Philosophical Dictionary*, trans. P. Gay (New York: Basic Books, Inc., 1962), 2:418; *The Work of Voltaire* (New York: The St. Hubert Guild, 1901), 2/2:140ff., 145, 155, 159; *Oeuvres Complètes de Voltaire* (Paris: Garnier Frères, Libraires-Éditeurs, 1879), 24:439.

3. *Ibid.*, 1:57, 220-221; 2:354-355, 366, 419, 432-433, 445.

4. *Oeuvres Complètes*, 24:75-77, 439ff., 449-453; 26:298-300; *Philosophical Dictionary*, 2:413-415, 485.

5. *Ibid.*, 24:445, 453; *Philosophical Dictionary*, 1:93-95, 105, 220, 238-244, 271-276; 2:347, 479.

6. *The Life and Selected Writings of Thomas Jefferson*, ed. A. Koch and W. Eden (New York: The Modern Library, 1944), 214-215, 719; *The Political Writings of Thomas Jefferson*, ed. E. Dumbauld (Indianapolis and New York: Bobbs-Merrill Co., 1955), 7-8.

7. *The Jefferson Cyclopedia*, ed. J. P. Foley (New York: Funk & Wagnalls Co., 1900), 745 (7257); *Political Writings*, 36, 50; *The Life and Selected Writings*, 431-432, 703, 706-707; *Writings* (New York: The Library of America, 1984), 1081, 1302.

8. *Writings*, 1124-1125, 1301-1302, 1373, 1437; *The Life and Selected Writings*, 570, 597, 694.

9. *The Writings of Thomas Jefferson*, ed. A. A. Lipscomb and A. E. Bergh (Washington, DC: The Thomas Jefferson Memorial Association, 1903), 15:245; *The Life and Selected Writings*, 555, 570, 694; *Writings*, 1213-1214. He considers Calvinism to be "daemonism" and the most bigotted form of religion. See *The Life and Selected Writings, 705-706; Writings, 1459, 1464*.

10. *Political Writings*, 72; *The Life and Selected Writings*, 430-431.

11. *Cyclopedia*, 744-745 (7244-7249, 7253); *Writings*, 510, 519-520, 1087, 1187, 1404. He does not even believe that preachers should address political concerns from the pulpit. Of course, it was Roger Williams who first spoke of the "wall of separation" between church and state long before Jefferson.

12. L. W. Levy, *Jefferson & Civil Liberties: The Darker Side*, 18, 35, 49-51, 59, 70-71, 158; *The Writings of Thomas Jefferson*, 7:460.

13. D. N. Mayer, *The Constitutional Thought of Thomas Jefferson* (Charlottesville and London: University Press of Virginia, 1994), 160, 165; J. B. Conant, *Thomas Jefferson and the Development of American Public Education* (Berkeley and Los Angeles: University of California Press, 1963), 3, 7, 13, 64.

14. *Writings*, 467, 477-479; *The Life and Selected Writings*, 725-726; Levy, *Jefferson & Civil Liberties*, 9-12, 144-150, 153, 156.

15. *Journal of the Senate of the Commonwealth of Virginia; Begun and Held in the City of Richmond on Monday, the 19th day of October, . . . , 1789, . . .* (Richmond: Thomas W. White, 1828), 62.

16. It was not until 1940 that the Supreme Court applied the Fourteenth Amendment to the First in *Cantwell v. Connecticut*. In this case the Court overturned the conviction of a Jehovah's Witness, who failed to obtain a license to proselyte his faith.

17. *Everson v. Board of Education*, 330 US 8-11, 16, 31.

18. *McCollum v. Board of Education*, 333 US 205-206, 211-212, 218.

19. *Lemon v. Kurtzman*, 403 US 612-616, 620, 625.

20. *Stone v. Graham*, 449 US 41-42.

21. "Approximately 12 percent of American children attend private schools, (the number as of 1991 hovered somewhere above 5 million) and, of those, 85 percent attend religious schools. . . ." S. L. Carter, *The Culture of Disbelief* (New York: Anchor Books, 1993), 195.

22. *McCollum v. Board of Education*, 333 US 203. Justice Jackson in a concurring opinion found the argument about the dissenter's embarrassment to have no basis in constitutional law. Teachers do not present their material with detached objectivity, and those who disagree will always feel a sense of alienation. 333 US 232-233, 236.

23. *Pierce v. Society of the Sisters*, 268 US 534. In order to have textbooks adopted in a state, publishers must show how their texts address a number of ethical and moral concerns of the state like good citizenship, patriotism, capitalism, individual rights, multiculturalism, etc. Nord, *Religion and American Education*, 334-335.

24. M. J. Behe, *Darwin's Black Box* (New York: Touchstone, 1996), 250.

25. *Summa Theologiae* (New York: McGraw-Hill, 1964-1976), I, q. 68, a.1; q. 72, a.1.

26. *Church Dogmatics*, III/1, 80-87, 100ff.

27. *Edwards v. Aguillard*, 482 US 581, 587, 603-607. In a dissenting opinion, Justice Scalia and the Chief Justice contended that religious motives do not automatically discredit legislation and the state does have the right to act against hostility to religion. William Nord notes that there are no references to creationism or counterarguments to the theory of evolution in the textbooks he studied, even though 30 percent of high school biology teachers according to a national survey are creationists. *Religion and American Education*, 155, 288.

28. Montesquieu, *The Spirit of the Laws*, 1.4.5(36).

29. M. McConnell, "Academic Freedom in Religious Colleges and Universities" *Law and Contemporary Problems* 53 (Summer 1990), 315.

30. *Philosophy and the Mirror of Nature* (Princeton: Princeton University Press, 1980), 178-179, 212, 299, 326-327, 371-372, 392-394; *Consequences of Pragmatism (Essays: 1972-1980)* (Minneapolis: University of Minnesota Press, 1982), 221.

31. *Consequences of Pragmatism*, xiv-xvi, xxvi, xlii-xliii; *Philosophy and the Mirror of Nature*, 12-13, 126, 170ff., 299-300, 330-332.

32. *Doing What Comes Naturally* (Durham and London: Duke University Press, 1992), 13, 245, 291, 395-396, 519.

33. *Ibid.*, 20-21, 176, 226-230, 304, 350-351, 420, 432-433, 496ff.

34. *Thus Spoke Zarathustra*, trans. R. J. Hollingdale (Great Britain: Penguin Books, 1978), 31, 41ff., 52, 61, 85; *Beyond Good and Evil*, trans. H. Zimmern (New York: The Modern Library, 1964), 88, 117, 135-136, 201; *The Twilight of the Idols . . . The Antichrist . . .*, trans. A. M. Ludovici (Edinburgh & London, 1915), 128ff., 202-204.

35. *The Antichrist*, 135, 230.

CHAPTER IV

Left v. Right

America is a deeply religious country, at least in accordance with its outward profession. According to Gallup polls, 94 percent of its people believe in God—a number that has not changed appreciably since the 1930s when Gallup began to take its polls on religion. More than half of Americans consider religion to be "very important" in their lives, while another 31 percent consider it "fairly important." Sixty-five percent are members of a local church or synagogue, and 41 percent attend one of these institutions on a regular basis. This is markedly in contrast to European countries with which most Americans share a common religious heritage. Less than half of Europeans believe in a personal God, and regular church attendance for Europeans is also less than half that of their American counterparts—West Germany (21 percent), Great Britain (14 percent), and France (12 percent).[1]

At the very beginning of America and throughout most of its history, the educational institutions of the country reflected strong religious beliefs. The colleges and universities of today were the stepchildren of Protestant churches and were under their auspices during their early years. Before the Civil War, "most college presidents, trustees, and faculty were ministers whose appointment depended on their beliefs." Even as late as the 1870s, most campuses were led by clergymen-presidents, who defended the Christian faith and encouraged spiritual revival and commitment among the student body. The president usually taught a required course in moral philosophy, which served as the capstone to the curriculum for seniors. It instilled a common set of Christian values, defended the faith, inculcated its truth, and applied that truth to the rest of the curriculum. As late as the 1890s, almost all state universities provided chapel services and required the attendance of the student body. The vast majority of the faculty were Christians and served in local churches as preachers, teachers, and administrators. According to James Angell, President of Yale University in the 1920s, 71 percent of professors at state universities were members of local congregations, and many of those not affiliated with a specific denomination were regarded as actively religious men.[2]

However, this all began to change at the end of the nineteenth century. In the decades that followed, schools began to retreat from their religious heritage. The boards, the faculty, and the administrations became peopled with laymen instead of clergymen, and explicit reference to the Scripture or theological matters was expunged from the curriculum. There were several reasons. One, education was becoming more the domain of the public at the end of the century. In accordance with the vision of Thomas Jefferson, this meant a necessary reducing of their religious nature. Two, universities were moving on their own toward a non-sectarian, Protestant approach in order to attract a wider, more diverse constituency. This nonsectarian approach might have some vague Christian reference and moral idealism to instill, but it could easily be watered down and then evaporate without anyone noticing the difference. Three, many American scholars were studying abroad at universities in Germany, which served as a graduate school for the nation in the nineteenth century, and were imbibing the liberal positions of their professors. Liberalism reached its zenith in Germany at the end of the nineteenth and beginning of the twentieth century before World War I shattered its illusions. Liberal beliefs served in their heyday as a direct assault upon the Calvinistic hegemony in America and went on to question most of the Christian heritage as it was historically received and interpreted by the church as a whole. By the end of the 1920s, the colleges and universities had become inhospitable to their forefathers, and evangelical or traditional Christian beliefs were effectively excluded from participating in any meaningful way in the future of American education.[3]

A good example of this transition is Harvard, the oldest school of higher education in the country. Harvard was founded in 1636 by the General Court of the Massachusetts Bay Colony. It was named after a Puritan minister, John Harvard, who bequeathed to the school his library of some four hundred volumes and half of his estate. While it had no specific statement of faith, the clergy and magistrates who made up the Board of Overseers insured that the interests of the Puritan community were served in both the spiritual and temporal spheres. About half of its graduates entered the ministry in the seventeenth century, and the ones who did not were instructed in the typical, Protestant work ethic of the day, which considered any vocation a sacred duty before God. Daily prayer and scriptural reading were prescribed for all students, while the weekend was devoted to biblical exposition and theology.[4]

Eventually in the nineteenth century the school was arrested from Puritan control, and its clerical and political connections dissipated. In 1805, a Unitarian (anti-trinitarian) minister became a professor of divinity, which marked the beginning of a close association between the school and left-wing, Unitarian thinking; in 1843, the board of overseers was opened to clergymen of all denominations; in 1865, the alumni began to elect its own members to the governing board; and in 1886, compulsory prayer and worship were dropped. The spiritual moorings were severed, and the school began to represent the opposite.

Today, the founding fathers would no longer recognize the school. Harvard is presently noted for its left-wing, avant-garde ideologies, which have little to do with their Puritan heritage and are antagonistic to traditional values of the culture at large and the church in particular. Even its Divinity School represents this anti-Christian posture. The Washington Times quoted a divinity student as saying, "Pluralism is the God at Harvard. The basic presumption is that Western religion is not good, and Christianity is the worst. The new slur, like being 'homophobic,' is being 'christo-centric.'" Another student disparaged the left-wing propaganda, saying,

> I learned word games. Capitalism, patriarchy, Christianity, patriotism, America, tradition, Republican, hierarchy—these were bad words. Feelings, liberation, oppression, victimization, conversations, dialogue, caucus, and empowerment were good words.[5]

Ari L. Goldman confirms much of this analysis in a book published in 1991, *The Search for God at Harvard*. Goldman was a reporter for the *New York Times* when he was given a Sabbatical leave to study religion at Harvard Divinity School. He was reared in the orthodox tradition of Judaism but became more flexible in regard to its strict, legal interpretations and came to appreciate the type of interfaith dialogue that Harvard had to offer. However, upon completing a year of study at the school he felt that his education was not complete. The school tended to "embrace religious relativism more than religious truth," and it did not represent the passions or commitment of America. "[T]he Div School brand of ultraliberal Christianity did not represent the faith, belief or politics of most Christians in the United States." He took a course on Catholicism, which he found to be more anti-Catholic in tenor and perspective. "Few Catholic thinkers, in fact, escaped the wrath of the instructor and her students." He found that Protestant Evangelicalism, "the most dynamic and vital force in Christianity," was largely ignored, and when mentioned, it received the utmost contempt and scorn of the professors. The whole school tended to embrace the liberal doctrine of tolerance toward different expressions of faith, except when it came to these conservatives. Its tolerance is extended to a host of multicultural forms, as long as they oppose the *ancien régime* of white males, Judeo-Christian ethics, the main line church, and the Bible.[6]

To illustrate these concerns let us take two of the school's leading figures, Harvey Cox and Elisabeth Schüssler Fiorenza, as representative of this left-wing posture. Cox is a professor in the Divinity School with a particular interest in the relationship between theological, social, and political issues. He is well-known for a book that he published in the 1960s entitled *The Secular City*. In this work, Cox rejoiced over what he described as the secularization and profanation of American society. He wrote that our society is becoming more and more this-worldly and is losing all need for the mythical and metaphysical meanings that were provided by its religious past. Religion has been relativized, privatized, and made innocuous in the modern world, and contrary to typical, Christian sensibilities, this is to be commended. Christians who attempt to fight this process are mistaken. Secularization is actually liberation. "Man must now assume responsibility for his world. He can no longer shove it off on some religious power."[7] (In this he joins many atheists in contending that a God who would emasculate the human race of its freedom and responsibility deserves to be dethroned. Secularization is therefore a means of placing our destiny in our own hands and allowing us to become the masters of our own fate. God is not necessary to the process. All that is needed is faith in our own abilities.)[8]

Cox goes on to commend the administration of John F. Kennedy for leading the country away from its "Protestant cultural hegemony" and toward the process of secularization. Prayer and Bible reading were exorcized from the public schools during Kennedy's administration, and Cox concurs with this decision. Religion has no place in the public arena. The task of all Christians is to join their President and his administration in demythologizing the country and insuring a secular future. Secularization, if anything, is the true message of the Christian Gospel. The church's role should be that of an exorcist, casting out the demons of our archaic, religious past and its superstitious illusions; and not only past beliefs but all remnants of transcendent and traditional values. Cox hoped to rid society of metaphysics all together. He believes that those who experience this big, beautiful world and rub shoulders with its diverse cultures will necessarily expand their horizons and question their traditional, provincial views. Things certainly are different in the secular city than what they are on the family farm. And so, in this brave new world, "diversity and the disintegration of tradition is paramount."[9]

Another leading figure at Harvard is Elizabeth Schüssler Fiorenza, a New Testament professor. She is noted for a book that was first published in 1983, *In Memory of Her: A Feminist Theological Reconstruction of Christian Origins*. In this book, she wished to reconstruct Christian history, where women are now hidden and invisible, and restore the rightful place they shared in its past. She contended that the Bible is a product of a patriarchal culture and needs redacting. The Bible is certainly not a neutral work, written from a divine perspective, when it comes to female issues but bears the imprint of the men who wrote it and contains prejudices against women, which one would find throughout Graeco-Roman culture. These prejudices have been used as a weapon against female liberation ever since. While some feminists recognize this and try to separate the essence of the biblical message from its cultural stamp, Fiorenza does not believe that this is possible. The Bible cannot be accepted at face value or demythologized to find some deeper, spiritual essence. It must only be read in light of feminist objections to it. The canon or measure of the faith must not be found in the Bible but in feminism or whatever promotes "the liberation of women from oppressive patriarchal texts."[10]

An example of her program is provided in the very title of the work, *In Her Memory*. The phrase comes from the Gospel of Mark (14:9). In the context, Jesus was reclining at a table in the home of Simon the Leper, who lived in Bethany. A certain woman, who is not identified by name, comes with an alabaster jar of very expensive perfume and proceeds to anoint the head of Jesus with the perfume. Some who are present complain that this is an extravagance—the perfume was worth a year's wages and could have been sold to feed the poor—but Jesus will have none of this. He rebukes the curmudgeons and commends the "beautiful thing" that the woman had done, anointing His body for burial. He says that wherever the Gospel is preached in the world, what she has done this day will be told "in memory of her." (Or at least that is what the patriarchal text would have us believe.)

The real story according to Fiorenza is much different. First, Jesus was mistaken. The woman's story has been virtually forgotten in the proclamation of the Gospel. The one who denied Jesus and the one who betrayed Him have always been afforded a more prominent role in its proclamation than this godly woman. Second, even her name is missing from the text. The reason behind the omission must be attributed to the patriarchal prejudices of its author. "The name of the betrayer is remembered, but the name of the faithful disciple is forgotten, because she was a woman." Whereas the Gospel of John does go on to identify the woman as Mary of Bethany, this reference is too little, too late. Third, Mark's account appears to have mitigated the importance of the woman's action. According to Fiorenza's version, the real story does not have the woman grabbling at Jesus' feet (cf. Luke 7:36ff.) and merely preparing her Master for burial but anointing the head of Jesus much like a prophet of old, who smeared oil on the head of Jewish kings. Through this "prophetic action-sign," she was proclaiming that Jesus was the Messiah (the "anointed one") of Israel, just as Peter had done previously in Mark 13. However, in contrast to Peter's rather hollow confession, this woman understood the nature of the messianic office to involve suffering and death, and so she has greater insight than the other, dim-witted males. Fiorenza does admit that her reconstruction of the text and others like it requires a certain amount of imagination, but this should not curtail our attempts to resurrect our sisters from oblivion and promote the feminist agenda.[11]

Unfortunately, Harvard is not alone in turning education into a left-wing propaganda machine. The positions of Cox and Fiorenza are all-too-characteristic of most colleges and universities, especially the older and more prestigious ones. Donald Kagan, Dean of Arts and Sciences at Yale, says, "It is common in universities today to hear talk of politically correct opinions, or PC for short. These are questions that are not really open to argument. It takes real courage to oppose the campus orthodoxy. To tell you the truth, I was a student during the days of McCarthy, and there is less freedom now than there was then." It is well-known that universities across the country inculcate a left-wing agenda in their students under the pretext of less offensive headings—inclusive language, multiculturalism, etc.—and at a number of these schools there are whole departments and curricula—minority studies, women's studies, etc.—which have been erected to instill the catechism. The administration of the schools not only encourages the propagation of this ideology but often discourages adverse opinions of any kind from the right as insensitive or harassment. Thomas Sowell, in his book *Inside American Education*, relates an incident at Dartmouth where several students were suspended for challenging the politically correct hegemony of the school. According to his report, they had the audacity to skate out onto the ice during the halftime of a Dartmouth hockey game, dressed in American Indian garb, in order to protest the politically correct motives of the administration in dropping the team's name, "Indians." The crowd cheered wildly at the sight and rose to sing the Alma Mater, but the administration was not so amused. It proceeded to sentence the entire student body to sensitivity training and suspended classes to do so. It also decided to suspend the three young "braves" from school a week before the end of the semester, and at least one of them was ordered to conduct public seminars on the evils of the Indian symbol and take an Indian to lunch once a week for a year, in order to expand his horizons.[12]

Most of the influence from the left-wing is not so obvious as these examples from Harvard and Dartmouth would indicate. Most often the influence subsists under the surface of academia in programs that would speak of much the opposite. In regard to religion, this comes in the form of what would seem to be so enlightened and so open to the world at large, the study of world religions, but the reality attests to a much different agenda. Religion departments began to grow dramatically after World War II, doubling in number between 1945 and 1960, and by the 1970s nearly all the universities in the country included them among their offerings. The study of world religions became more and more the basic focus of these departments through the years, as they moved away from the advancement of Christianity toward the acknowledgment of all religious forms. On the surface, it would seem that they were conducting a quest for God throughout the world, but in reality they became a bastion for some of the most anti-western and anti-Christian relativism throughout our universities. (Unlike a science department, which seeks to advance our knowledge, religion departments prefer to patronize third world superstitions as worthy of our interest—all in the name of relativism. A medical school would never patronize a shaman or witch doctor, but religion departments are more than willing to do whatever it takes. The prevailing dogma is that there are no dogmas, so each religion must be seen as good as the next in expressing whatever grand mystery is out there.)[13]

The dogma of multiculturalism clearly stands in conflict with the basic tenor of the Judeo-Christian tradition. From its very beginning, the Jewish faith stood opposed to the worship of other gods before Yahweh. It refused to find the true and living God in the idols and images of their neighbors. It refused to limit God to one place as if he represented the power of a particular region or a force in nature. There was one God, who ruled over all the heavens and the earth, and this God could not become captive to a specific form or power. He alone was God.

The monotheism of Israel was clearly opposed to the multicultural practices of the day. The neighbors of ancient Israel were more than willing to adopt whatever religious system they found in an area and worship its gods. The Philistines, when they migrated from Crete to Palestine, did not merely import their own strange gods to the land but worshiped Dagon, the god who already occupied the territory. Moving to a new land meant assimilating the new gods who inhabited the new region.[14]

This practice continued to flourish during New Testament times. The Romans assimilated the gods of the Greek pantheon when they conquered the Greek kingdom. Apologists of Graeco-Roman culture like Celsus thought it odd that Jews and Christians could not find their one, true God in the many names and images of the Mediterranean world. The apologists of the time found it particularly repugnant that Christians proclaimed themselves as the Way—an early name for the sect found in the book of Acts. Christians proclaimed that Jesus of Nazareth, a man who suffered an ignominious death on a cross, was the Messiah of Israel and the one, true Savior of the world. Peter said that salvation was found in no other name (Acts 4:12)—a dogma that irked the multiculturalists of the day and still causes great division today.[15]

Of course, this does not mean that the liberal community is free from its own dogma. The American brand of multiculturalism has clear limits on what fits within its agenda and can be tolerated in the twentieth century. It does not accept or interact with that which runs counter to its own basic assumptions. It is not interested in interacting with the Hindu concept of women—feminism is its dogma. It is not interested in the caste system—egalitarianism is its truth. And it is certainly not interested in conservative Christians participating in any meaningful way in its dialogue. The Scripture if it is mentioned at all must be taught by those who employ the most sophisticated, higher critical techniques, in order to discredit whatever special or unique authority it might possess for those who reject relativity.

A number of studies have examined this issue and found a decided bias against traditional, religious expressions at American colleges and universities. Despite all the calls for diversity in our society, these studies do not find the devoutly religious represented among the faculty of these campuses, nor do they find their ideas afforded equal opportunity in the classroom. The inclusiveness of the left has come to mean the exclusion of more conservative, religious forms from their orbit. It has come to mean that a wide range of different types of liberals—liberal females, liberal Blacks, liberal Jews, etc.—are to be tolerated, but it does not include a serious plurality of ideological perspectives. Taxes are now spent in this country not to support religion, but to promote the opposite.

Anyone familiar with the literature can recognize bias. Most college books and texts are replete with examples. Stewart Cole, in his *History of Fundamentalism,* says that the conservatives' "inferiority in scholarship" is only "compensated for in his sense of superiority in spiritual status, and this condition of mind permits him to engage *ex animo* in any diatribe he pleases against open-minded seekers for the truth that sets men free." Norman F. Furniss claims that these people align themselves "against ideas that (have) the weight of fact behind them" and believe that they can only employ "coercion to still their opponents without granting opportunity for open exchange of opinion." Richard Hofstadter asserts in his book, *Anti-intellectualism in American Life,* that conservatives possess a "generically prejudiced mind. Studies of political intolerance and ethnic prejudice have shown that zealous church-going and rigid religious faith are among the important correlates of political and ethnic animosity." Noam Chomsky disparages the conservative religious beliefs of most Americans as worthy of "mosques in Iran" and "old ladies in Sicily."[16]

These and other examples are cited by studies to speak of the bias against conservatives in education. In a most recent and comprehensive study of this matter, George Marsden concludes his study with the following comments:

> In many of the American colonies all the citizens were taxed for the support of the established religious group, regardless of the citizens' religious affiliations. In the nineteenth century the Protestant establishment became informal and declared itself nonsectarian. Today nonsectarianism has come to mean the exclusion of all religious concerns. In effect, only purely naturalistic viewpoints are allowed a serious academic hearing. As in earlier establishments, groups who do not match the current national ideological norms are forced to fend for themselves outside of the major spheres of cultural influence. Today, almost all religious groups, no matter what their academic credentials, are on the outside of this educational establishment, or soon will be, if present trends continue. Americans who are concerned for justice ought to be open to considering alternatives.[17]

Religious liberalism first began to assert itself in higher education at the beginning of the nineteenth century. It was Friedrich Schleiermacher who set much of the agenda for liberal education in those early years. Schleiermacher helped to lead liberalism and the academic community into rejecting the traditional church's concept of Christ and the Bible as a special and unique revelation from God. He said that there are no special acts or miracles by which God discloses Himself to a limited few at a certain time and place. God does not reveal Himself specifically to some or perform special acts of wonder apart from nature, as witnessed by the miracles of the Bible. He is not found in a limited space and time but is revealed everywhere within the whole system of nature and is available for all to see. The only "miracle" that occurs is within our hearts, when we discover in nature the presence of God—a God who was there all along. All of humanity, he said, are born with this capacity to find God. All they need to do is look deep within, not to the sin nature or total depravity of orthodox teaching, but to uncover the truth that is reflected within our spirits and its feelings. We are all born with this inner impulse toward God-consciousness, and as long as it is not impeded it should well-up within us naturally. There is no metaphysical evil to be found within or without—no sin nature, no devil. "All that is human is holy, for all is divine." God is an immanent force in the world, which is reflected in all events and all people, no matter how natural or pagan. All religions reflect from their diverse field of vision the same feeling of absolute dependence upon God, which is the true essence of religion, and while Jesus might have been filled with this consciousness more than others and Christianity might be more highly evolved, the Christian faith is not qualitatively distinct from others. Jesus is only a man, not the incarnate God, and Christianity does not possess a monopoly upon God's time or His salvation.[18]

The liberal community followed Schleiermacher's work with a number of critical studies to discredit the traditional view of Scripture and provide "scientific" credence for its own theories. In Old Testament studies, Julius Wellhausen published its most celebrated analysis, *Prolegomena to the History of Ancient Israel* (1883), providing the basic outline for a liberal, yet scholarly view of the Old Testament. He contended, based on his own liberal, enlightened thinking, that the history of Israel as recorded in the Bible must have been redacted or edited by later priests, in order to enslave the masses to their own religious devices. The real history of ancient Israel did not include what we have under its name in our present Bible—a centralized place of worship, a detailed legal code, or a sacrificial system of atonement—means that priests employ to wield their power. In ancient Israel, the religious festivals were rooted in the land, not historical redemption, and the sacrifices were a simple meal with Jehovah, unentangled with thoughts of paying atonement to God or dues to a priesthood. The worship was natural, spontaneous, and local. It was free and liberal, just like any son of liberalism would want it.[19] It was free from the power of priests, just like Voltaire, Wellhausen, and any son of the Enlightenment would wish.

In New Testament studies, David Strauss provided the most celebrated and influential work of liberalism in his *Life of Jesus* (1835). This work attempted to discover what all liberal Christians wish to find and follow—the historical Jesus. However, the account of Jesus as recorded in the four Gospels cannot be trusted or followed at face value, because it contains matters that are offensive to liberal sensibilities and must therefore be discarded as unscientific. There are two matters that particularly incur the wrath of Strauss and all liberals in their attempt to reconstruct the life of Jesus, the miracle stories and the messianic prophecies, which He allegedly fulfilled. Both of these must be excised from an account of the true life of Jesus, because any talk of divine intervention into time and space contradicts what Strauss believes in most, the steady state of natural law or, perhaps better, the Newtonian concept of the universe as a self-perpetuating machine—a concept so prevalent in the nineteenth century. Any special revelation or intervention of God in history must be considered a scientific impossibility, and all the narratives of Scripture that contain miraculous healings or predictions must be expunged from the text as later interpolations of the church. It was the church in their overzealous, apologetic fervor to make Jesus more than what He was that added these accounts to His life. But the real Jesus did not heal people with divine power or fulfill prophecies of old concerning the Messiah. He was not the incarnate God or resurrected Lord, the Savior or the Messiah, of later Christian orthodoxy. His only "miracles" were spiritual or moral in nature as He inspired the disciples to follow His example. He provided in His person an ideal pattern of gentleness and kindness for all of humanity to follow in the coming age. The real Jesus was a simple, moral teacher, and that is all—all that a liberal like Strauss wanted. His scientific criticism eliminated all the other elements that conservatives or the traditional church had sought in the life of Jesus, or so it seemed to Strauss.[20]

In the twentieth century, however, the scientific status of the liberal enterprise was called into question. The liberal religion that emerged in Germanic realms was severely chastened on a number of fronts and became less dogmatic than it was during its heyday in Schleiermacher, Wellhausen, and Strauss. Albert Schweitzer attempted in *The Quest for the Historical Jesus* (1906) to find the ethical leader of the liberal community through his own critical analysis. Instead, he found that scholars like Strauss would dismiss elements from the text of the Gospels as unhistorical for no apparent reason beyond their own religious prejudices. For example, Jesus as portrayed in the Gospels was clearly caught up in the apocalyptic fervor of His day in word and deed, but scholars dismissed this element as unhistorical because it could not be reconciled with what they themselves believed. The Jesus who emerged from these studies was more what they wanted, "a phantom created by the Germanic mind," a "Jesus (made) after its own likeness," than anything the text would warrant. Jesus had become a receptacle into which theologians wished to pour their ideas, in order to receive some blessing from Him for what they believed as a religious "founder" for their own, man-made religion. In the case of Strauss, Jesus had become a nineteenth century, post-Kantian liberal, one who would quite naturally reduce religion to morality; but this, of course, was most unlikely. Schweitzer said that it would be better for those who cling to modern ideals to send Jesus back to His own time and recognize that Jesus is a stranger to our own. No method of critical study can separate from the text with any degree of confidence the natural from the supernatural, the ancient from the modern, the Jesus of history from the Christ of faith.[21]

Today postmodernism has come to question the scientific nature of the liberal humanities in general. Michel Foucault, in his scintillating analysis of the human sciences, wishes to display that much of what is held with such dogmatic fervor by left-wing intellectuals arose from rather arbitrary constraints in the past. Often what is believed today is a construct of bizarre or fortuitous twists and turns in history, which speak little of scientific necessity, display the arbitrary use of power, and can be criticized and discredited on this basis. The rituals of truth that they hold so dear are a product, not of scientific rigor, but the demands and interests of capricious events and acts of power in the past. For example, in his analysis of psychology, Foucault complains that madness was not treated as a "mental illness" in the fifteenth and sixteenth centuries when Erasmus wrote his *Praise of Folly*. It became constituted as such only later on through a power play of the psychological community. They are the ones who constituted madness a disease in the name of their science. However, much of this so-called scientific analysis was a product of the unfortunate association in history of the mad with the guilty. In the seventeenth century, madmen, the immoral, and criminals were all incarcerated together. But the madmen, who were often treated like animals (chained to the floor, denied bedding, etc.), began to drive everyone in the facility crazy through their sleepless nights and wailing, and the insane asylum arose in order to separate them from the regular criminals. Nevertheless,

Foucault maintains that a guilt-by-association emerged from those days. Since the mad were once incarcerated with the guilty, they too began to share the burden of the other prisoners. This guilt was considered the product not so much of overt acts since they were not actual criminals but became internalized within their souls through the constitution of their society. And so, psychology arose to treat this disease in their souls, and its origin is not to be found in simple, scientific analysis but within the moralization that was produced from a fortuitous association of the madmen with criminals. "What is called psychiatric practice (today) is a certain moral tactic . . . overlaid with myths of positivism," i.e., the myths of science.[22]

Stanley Fish considers much of what falls under the rubric of academia to involve nothing beyond the arbitrary use of power. In a brilliant essay, "Withholding the Mission Portion: Psychoanalysis and Rhetoric," Fish follows much of what Foucault says in his treatment of psychoanalytic theory. He believes that this type of analysis involves nothing more than an authoritarian act of pure rhetoric or persuasion. Its founder, Sigmund Freud, particularly embodied this spirit in the autocratic posture that he assumed toward those who fell under his spell. Freud was known to be an insufferable, egotistical maniac, who considered every colleague and patient who dared to disagree with him neurotic. Freud's strong arm, bully-boy tactics demanded belief from everyone. The patients who rejected his authority or analysis were considered to be "in denial." The colleagues who doubted his detailed and bizarre analysis of dreams simply did not possess the ability to penetrate into the deeper recesses of the human psyche, discover the sexual fantasies that lurk beneath the surface, and discern the inevitable, scientific logic of the Freudian way. The profession today, in fact, is notorious for creating through divination and bizarre insights previously unknown conditions for its patients and multiplying heterogeneities in our society.[23]

However, Fish does not wish to limit his rather disparaging analysis just to psychology and the other "soft" sciences but believes that even the "hard" sciences should be disparaged as engaging in nothing more than the fine art of persuasion. Here he basically defers to the well-received analysis of Thomas Kuhn in *The Structure of the Scientific Revolution* (1962). In this work, Kuhn disparages the typical, scientific textbook of the day, which would depict science as a triumphant, linear march toward the truth. Science, he says, does not develop through the accumulation of individual discoveries or inventions in a developmental line toward the truth. "Progress" is made in science only when a new paradigm declares absolute victory, and the past is mentioned in a distorted way as if leading up to its discovery. But this is an act of faith. The new paradigm does not explain it all. It is accepted by a group that has become particularly enthralled with its success in explaining a certain set of problems with which they are intrigued, while ignoring all else. The scientists who will go on to accept the paradigm often assemble facts to prove its worth or fine-tune its perceptions but serve as little more than pawns in its hands. The theory has already told them how to look at the world, and the facts or results of any subsequent experiment are already dictated or interpreted by the theory. Both fact and theory belong together. They cannot be separated. A new theory only "requires the reconstruction of prior theory and the re-evaluation of prior fact."[24] As an example, Kuhn contends that it is difficult to state when oxygen was first discovered, since the element itself changes with every shift in paradigm.

> Was it Priestley or Lavoisier, if either, who first discovered oxygen? In any case, when was oxygen discovered? In that form the question could be asked even if only one claimant had existed. As a ruling about priority and date, an answer does not at all concern us. Nevertheless, an attempt to produce one will illuminate the nature of discovery, because there is no answer of the kind that is sought. Discovery is

not the sort of process about which the question is appropriately asked. The fact that it is asked—the priority for oxygen has repeatedly been contested since the 1780s—is a symptom of something askew in the image of science that gives discovery so fundamental a role. Look once more at our example. Priestly's claim to the discovery of oxygen is based upon his priority in isolating a gas that was later recognized as a distinct species. But Priestley's sample was not pure, and, if holding impure oxygen in one's hands is to discover it, that had been done by everyone who ever bottled atmospheric air. Besides, if Priestley was the discoverer, when was the discovery made? In 1774 he thought he had obtained nitrous oxide, a species he already knew; in 1775 he saw the gas as dephlogisticated air, which is still not oxygen or even, for phlogistic chemists, a quite unexpected sort of gas. Lavoisier's claim may be stronger, but it presents the same problems. If we refuse the palm to Priestly, we cannot award it to Lavoisier for the work of 1775 which led him to identify the gas as the "air itself entire." Presumably we wait for the work of 1776 and 1777 which led Lavoisier to see not merely the gas but what the gas was. Yet even this award could be questioned, for in 1777 and to the end of his life Lavoisier insisted that oxygen was an atomic "principle of acidity" and that oxygen gas was formed only when that "principle" united with caloric, the matter of heat. Shall we therefore say that oxygen had not yet been discovered in 1777? Some may be tempted to do so. But the principle of acidity was not banished from chemistry until after 1810, and caloric lingered until the 1860s. Oxygen had become a standard chemical substance before either of those dates.[25]

In religion, the demise of the scientific status of its discipline led many in Germanic realms to abandon the quest for the historic Jesus entirely and recognize the theological nature of whatever they said academically. Many of the theologians who appeared after World War I made a decided turn to the right and rejected the liberal ideas of their mentors, which, they felt, were partially responsible for the war. Today there subsists, because of these developments, more breadth of opinion between the left and the right in the country, at least more than what one would find in America today.

The hegemony of liberalism, while chastened by the developments in some respects, still remains as strong as ever in America. The most popular textbook in the New Testament, for example, is Spivey and Smith's *Anatomy of the New Testament*—a text which deals with many of the historical questions previously mentioned and reflects much of the same liberal, scientific spirit. While more humble in force than Strauss, its subtleties do not conceal its overall, liberal agenda in the end. The authors present their work as the product of critical scholarship, not "dogmatic desire," but their own dogmatic agenda is clearly on display throughout the work. It is clear that they wish to reject the church's portrait of Jesus Christ as seen in the Gospels and its confessions and maintain that it cannot be merged with the Jesus of history. According to Spivey and Smith and "most critical scholars," Jesus did not conceive of Himself as a Savior, suffering a vicarious death for the sins of His people, as orthodoxy reports. The sayings in the Gospels that would portray Jesus in this way must be considered the unhistorical product of the later church's redaction. Jesus did not say, "For even the Son of Man did not come to be served but to serve, and give His life as a ransom for many" (Mark 10:45; Matt. 10:28). And not only is this statement an historical falsification, but also are all the claims in the Gospels that present Jesus as the Messiah of Israel or the only-begotten Son of God. Again these are attributed to the overzealous nature of the church, which attempted to make Jesus into more than what He claimed to be or possibly could be. In fact, the Gospels themselves are not the product of early witnesses at all, regardless of what the testimony of our earliest sources might say, for the very same reason that leads the textbook to reject the previous claim. "Critical scholarship" knows that Jesus could not have predicted the fall of Jerusalem and the destruction of its temple in 70 A.D. during His lifetime as the Gospels report, because Jesus is not God. Therefore, the Gospels must have been written just before (Mark) or some years after (Matthew, Luke, and John) this event, not by the original disciples or their hearers, but the later church, so that the church could be accused of feigning this prediction (i.e., putting it into Jesus' mouth) and be scorned for having no historical basis to their claim of His divine origin.[26]

This type of analysis is typically found at universities in religion departments but is not representative of the religious sensibilities of the nation as a whole. America, despite the left-wing antagonism and best efforts of academia, describes itself as more conservative than liberal when it comes to religious matters in general. American belief in the divinity of Christ (84 percent) and personal commitment to Him (66 percent) remain strong and has even shown some signs of increase in recent years. Just over half of the people confess the full authority of the Bible, while another quarter consider its words to be "mostly true."[27]

In fact, much of the religious passion in the country is not centered in the liberal community but is found among those whom they despise the most, the Evangelicals, or what the press describes as "born-again" Christians. Gallup polls estimate that one-third of the nation consists of these people; including one-half of those who live in the South and one-half of all Protestants. They represent the most conservative and zealous members of the entire Christian community. In contrast to non-evangelicals, they rely on religious values for moral guidelines (56 to 34 percent), consider religion very important in their lives (84 to 40 percent), consider it essential to have a deeper relationship with God (94 to 45 percent), claim church membership (87 to 59 percent), and attend church on a regular, weekly basis (60 to 34 percent).[28]

These Christians, along with other conservatives in mainline denominations and religious groups, represent the true opponents of the liberal, religious agenda. The differences between liberals and conservatives have little to do with the historical reasons that divided the church of the past into its various denominations, but they do constitute what is most essential in distinguishing between groups within the church or in the religious community as a whole. It is often the case that a liberal Jew and a liberal Protestant have much more in common on religious matters than a liberal and a conservative have in their respective denominations or religious affiliations. Liberals can often feign diversity or pluralism by joining together all sorts of different faiths, but this seldom displays a serious attempt at an ideological spectrum of ideas and beliefs. The devoutly religious, the conservative and the orthodox, are not a part of their dialogue or ecumenical community. In fact, it is common knowledge that evangelical Christians are systematically excluded by them from participation in the religion departments of this country—a fact that few would deny and the Equal Employment Opportunity Commission (EEOC) seems to care little about.[29]

The exclusion of conservative ideals from the public domain is justified in the liberal mind-set because of the belief that liberal ideals contain the correct or scientific approach to the subject. Even if many of the greatest theological minds in the twentieth century—Barth, Brunner, Moltmann, Jüngel, and other German theologians—are fundamentally conservative, even if the majority of the religious community in this country is conservative, this does not prevent them from imposing their minority viewpoints on others or fighting with power the "evil" majority's "victimization" of the truth. (It is much the same as one would find in a liberal jurist, who believes that he or she is the vanguard of the constitution against the tyranny of the majority, or a left-wing political group who believes that totalitarian ideals are the decrees of a scientific, materialistic outlook.) Left-wing ideals must be imposed no matter what the conservative and the ignorant majority might prefer instead. William E. Hordern in *A Laymen's Guide to Protestant Theology* says,

> Far from dying out, various opinion polls indicate that the conservatives speak for a larger number of Protestant clergy and laity than does any other theological position. Conservatives are keen students of nonconservatives theology and are willing to learn from it. Nonconservatives are less willing to read and much less willing to learn from the conservatives.[30]

In his classic work *On Liberty* (1859), J. S. Mill extolled what liberals have long forgotten, the virtue of ideological diversity as the mark of a free society. There is no doubt that our deeply divided religious community, as well as the nation as a whole, could profit from reading this lesson once again. While the country has moved toward a form of diversity in ethnic-and gender-related issues, it has also brought censorship to bear on those opinions that do not reflect the agenda or confess what is offensive to certain groups. Ideological diversity has been sacrificed for the sake of not offending the left or the rainbow coalition of its constituency, and because of this, the truth has become much more expendable than what a nation dedicated to pluralism desires. The truth, Mill says, is best served not through the triumph of a cause but through the continual struggle of opposite camps, who must scrape and scrap and strengthen their ideas. It is important to the truth that each element of an issue receive its just due—capitalism and communism, socialism and individualism, liberalism and conservatism—otherwise one side of the issue becomes godlike and fair play becomes null and void. It is only through the struggle of adverse opinions that each position is perfected and the truth is illuminated in their midst. Without a serious listening to the pros and cons no comprehension of the complexity of an issue can be obtained, or a nuanced and balanced position forged. A position that is condemned to silence can no longer speak for its truth, and the accepted position will become nothing but a prejudice, without rational basis, whose meaning has lost all vital force and whose profession is a mere formula.[31]

Serious thinking always requires the destruction of a single, monolithic rule of authority. Mill is particularly concerned about the exercise of this type of authority when the state becomes involved in education. "That the whole or any large part of the education of the people should be in State hands, I go as far as any one in deprecating." He feels that diversity of opinion and individuality of character involves diversity in our educational resources. State education finds its interests not in the diversity of truth but in molding people into a certain, politically correct image that it finds useful to its current agenda or concept of society. In the case of a democratic government, the majority or the politically active come to practice a form of despotism over the mind, which persecutes those who do not conform to what has been accepted by society as normative. The tyranny of prevailing opinions or the tendency of society to impose itself upon the entire citizenry compels conformity and destroys the individual eccentricities of creative minds, which are necessary in propelling a society onward to new frontiers.[32]

This danger is particularly acute in America. Alexis de Tocqueville, who wrote the most definitive work on this country in its early years, complained that "freedom of opinion does not exist in America." He thought that there was much greater diversity and freedom of discussion in Europe, where democratic forces were not so great. Little difference seemed to subsist in his mind between the way Americans thought about issues, at least when compared to the wide range of expression he found in Europe. Tocqueville blamed it on the enormous pressure that democracy exerted upon the citizens to conform to the prevailing opinion of the day and the fact that all institutions of the land were placed in its hands. "The majority raises formidable barriers around the liberty of opinion." One might find the freedom to speak one's mind without immediate peril to life and property, but one would also live as a stranger among the people and never be chosen for anything of substance unless one conformed to the prevailing orthodoxy.[33]

Today this orthodoxy is represented in religion by the liberal intelligentsia and a secular public, which have no fundamental devotion to religion and often demean those who do. The devoutly religious simply do not fit their image of what it is to be "cool" (and that is about as deep as it goes). While the devout represent a majority of those who attend church, study its message, and follow the cause, they are still in the minority when it comes to the prevailing power of liberal and secular forces, and can be shouted down in society at large with much ridicule.

The liberals do find honor in the secular world for this ridicule, but the effect it has on the religious community, which they also serve, is disastrous. The most arresting example of the destructive influence of liberalism can best be illustrated in the demise of the so-called mainline denominations. The seven sister churches that comprise these denominations are the American Baptist Churches in the USA, the Christian Church (Disciples of Christ), the Episcopal Church, the Evangelical Lutheran Church in America, the Presbyterian Church (USA), the United Church of Christ, and the United Methodist Church; and all of them have registered a significant downturn in their membership over the last few decades. In the 1950s, when going to church was what decent, middle class Americans were supposed to do, their numbers were growing and their fellowship robust. However, the cultural revolution of the 60s and 70s changed all that. While the constituency remained moderate in their beliefs, the hierarchy and the politically active began to drive the message of the church in accordance with the revolution toward a more liberal posture. The result was disastrous. Over the last three decades, while conservative churches have shown a dramatic growth rate, the mainline churches have begun the process of withering, graying, and dying. The United Methodist Church, for example, which boasted fifteen million members at one time in this past century, lost an average of one thousand members per week during this period of time and is now just over eight million, most of whom are fifty years of age and older. The same could be said of the other churches in its orbit.[34]

Liberalism is failing these churches and it is no great surprise. If a pastor patronizes the philosophy of pop culture, there is no need to go to church and hear the same message that is broadcast in the world all week long. One might as well stay home and watch MTV, which is more creative, entertaining, and shocking in its confrontation with traditional values. If the pastor does not preach a word that opposes the culture, why bother to escape its clutches? Why listen to a message from Scripture that can be interpreted however you want it, or is so filled with errors and nonsense as to be irrelevant to our modern way of thinking? Of course, the left-wing can serve a useful purpose in the church, especially as it confronts narrow-minded traditionalism and promotes the continual reformation of its beliefs. It serves a purpose in demythologizing traditional values, recognizing the complexity and temporal nature of all solutions, and remaining open to a world, which is ever-changing around us. Many of the theologians and books that were mentioned above as representative of left-wing bias are filled with these valuable insights from which all of us could profit. However, left to its own devices liberalism can deteriorate into pure cynicism and leave a church and a society in spiritual bankruptcy. Its rejection of time-tested tradition is often for the sake of embracing nothing at all, and if it confesses anything, it is often in behalf of something new—whatever is the latest fad, the most temporal, unproven craze of current culture—something that is sure to fade with the passing of time. Its strength might be found in its openness to criticism and change, but its weakness is related to its lack of serious confession. Any society needs more than this. Any society requires more than what liberalism can provide with its continual fluctuation with the times and its disregard for substantive, eternal truth.

However, the plight of conservative ideals in American society cannot be laid to the charge of liberalism exclusively. Conservatives at the beginning of this century contributed much to their own demise as they decided to leave society and live separately in their own institutions away from the corrupting influences of liberalism. J. Gresham Machen, a New Testament scholar from Princeton, became the most resounding and outspoken clarion of the call to separate. In his *Christianity and Liberalism* (1923), he called for complete separation from what he considered "a totally diverse type of religious belief from Christianity." Even if some liberals might be a part of God's kingdom, a matter that God alone can judge, "liberalism is not Christianity at all." It denies cardinal doctrines of the faith, despite its deceptive use of traditional terminology, and cannot be accepted into the fellowship of God's people. Machen's solution was to leave Princeton with all its valuable resources (its library, its endowment, its prestige, etc.), take along with him other like-minded professors, and form a separate, conservative school, Westminister Theological Seminary, as a bastion of true Christian orthodoxy. This move helped to precipitate a massive withdrawal by other conservatives from mainline denominations and schools. The result of this withdrawal can be seen in the deeply divided community that we have in America today; a community divided between extremes on both sides with liberals controlling the more public, mainline schools and conservatives the more private, separatist schools.[35]

As a part of separationism, conservative schools became intransigent in their various versions of orthodoxy. They sought to define themselves in such a way as to prevent liberalism from encroaching upon their schools, as it had done elsewhere in the society at large, but the result was an education that became impervious to self-doubt and self-criticism. They had the truth and knew it. Education was a matter of indoctrination into a certain form of faith or a matter of defending truth as it was already understood. As a result, they became subject to much criticism by the liberal community for being narrow-minded, self-righteous, and bigoted. The criticisms were perhaps unfair in some regards and certainly overexercised in most, but none of them were totally without merit.

In Protestantism, the belief in certitude was not the invention of the conservative wing in the twentieth century but actually goes back all the way to its founder, the great apostle of assurance, Martin Luther. Luther found assurance for his standing before God through a word of promise, and Protestantism merely expanded this certainty to include other areas of the Christian faith, including one's entire belief system during the age of orthodoxy. As a monk in the Catholic Church, Luther felt enslaved to the incessant performance of works—vigils, prayers, and fasts—which were supposed to bring favor before God but brought little more than fear and torment to his soul. His breakthrough came when he decided to stop dwelling on his own shortcomings in these matters and simply believe the word of absolution, which the priest spoke forth during the sacrament of confession. When the priest pronounced the simple formula "I absolve you," Luther believed that the priest was speaking for God and one could be assured of forgiveness as if receiving a personal word from God. In fact, Luther went on to demand absolute certitude from those who expected to receive forgiveness as a simple matter of faith. This certitude became a mark of all Protestantism thereafter, not only in regard to one's personal salvation but also in regard to whatever conviction they developed in matters of faith. All doubt was now considered sinful, and not only sinful but subject to eternal damnation.[36]

However, the Christian faith has never been lived in such a triumphant way within the real world of temptation and doubt. Even Luther spoke of the Christian life as caught between the power of Christ within and the old, worldly nature of human depravity, which continually vexed the soul with spiritual trials (*Anfechtung*) and anxiety (*Angst*). Paul

Tillich, a modern theologian, would go even farther and say that faith and doubt should be combined together as dialectical forces rather than torn apart as simple rivals. Faith, he says, does not possess an absolute knowledge of its object as if it could be separated from doubt. It lives in terms of possibilities, which it affirms in the midst of negative forces surrounding it. It resolves to live in spite of the forces that would negate it, and yet cannot live without the scepticism and other forces of non-being, which it chooses to resist.[37] In fact, the Bible, when it comes to speak of faith, does not refer to what is seen or known. It refers to what remains outside this world and invisible to the eye.

> Now faith is the assurance of things hoped for and the conviction of things not seen. . . . All those who believed of old were still living by faith when they died, even though they did not receive the things promised and only saw or welcomed them from a distance. (Heb. 11:1, 13)

Tillich believed that life in general is filled with the same kind of dialectical tensions or ambiguities. Simple knowledge would try to negate these tensions and develop a system, but it does so only by sacrificing whatever rivals its truth. It refuses to listen to the tensions anymore and prefers to create an artificial whole in its place. This ambiguity he relates to the struggles that rage between conservative and liberal camps in religion, politics, etc. The one side represents our sacred allegiance to the past and holds strongly to its ideals, while the other looks to change our beliefs in hope of creating a better tomorrow. Neither side represents the whole truth. Both contain their own aberrations. Destruction can only result when either side comes to power, claims victory, and asserts itself as ultimate.[38] Of course, policies must be forged, confessions made, and risks taken, but one should never venture to resolve a conflict without a certain amount of resignation or recognition of that which remains unspoken and undone. The risk of saying and doing can become a form of idolatry if it is not accompanied by the recognition that whatever step is taken in life can only represent a preliminary attempt in expressing what is ultimate. God is in heaven. We are on earth (Eccl. 5:2). We must remain open to God and place Him in the center of our devotion, not some immanent system of human construction or staple of doctrinal truth. There is no greater form of idolatry. There is no greater lie against the truth, no greater invention of the Antichrist—whether it is liberalism's all too auspicious equation of their current ideals with the historical Jesus or orthodoxy's adherence to the confessions of the past as the very Word of God.

A good example of aberrant, right-wing thinking is the so-called Reconstructionists. Many of them are graduates of Westminster Theological Seminary and hold to its fundamental catechism, the inerrancy of Scripture and the Westminster Confession. Greg Bahnsen, one of its leading theologians, says that within these standards there are contained exhaustive details and extensive, specific, and all-encompassing commands, by which a society or a person can determine whatever must be done in life. This, of course, particularly relates to the words of the Bible, which are said to be "immutable and eternal." They are considered by Bahnsen to be just as relevant today and perspicuous in nature as they were when the Scripture was first written down over three thousand years ago. They contain within its confines a simple recipe, which is clear to anyone who consults its pages and is so exhaustive as to include God's plain counsel on every area of life. One does not need to consult the Spirit or translate the message from the past to the present. The message means the same today as it did back then. The civil laws of the Old Testament are still just as applicable today as they were when God proclaimed His will to Moses and the children of Israel thousands of years ago. In fact, they were really not announced to them at all, but to all nations, all times, and all circumstances through them. When the law of Moses prescribes capital punishment to the Israelites for the following crimes—murder, adultery, sodomy, homosexuality, witchcraft, blasphemy, apostasy, etc.—we must follow and do likewise. We must promote this standard as the eternal will of God. We must even follow its method of punishment or penology. We must burn witches and stone adulterers in accordance with its mandates. Covenant theology as taught in the Westminster Confession does not allow us to interpret the Scripture in any other way or relegate its commands to bygone days. God's will does not change with time or circumstance, and we must follow its message to the letter.[39]

Mainline theologians of the Reformed faith would deny that its traditions must be interpreted in this way. Emil Brunner denies that absolute justice could present itself within a fallen world in such a simplistic manner. He contends that one should not cut oneself off from reality in an attempt to impose an absolute standard. All human codes must work within a certain set of circumstances and provide at best an approximate or relative semblance of justice in light of our fallen condition. One must adapt codes to existing historical conditions, not wishful thinking, and bring a sense of realism, which is not blinded by some fanatical sense of what would be perfect in a perfect world. One cannot, for example, outlaw divorce in society because it is against the order of creation. Jesus, who hated divorce more than others, admitted that it was necessary for God to allow His people to divorce in the Old Testament "because of the hardness of their hearts." They would not have it any other way. He could not outlaw divorce in Jewish society at that time considering the circumstances of the people and their spiritual condition.[40]

Besides, the commandments of God as recorded in Scripture are not universal in nature. They are filled out in concrete situations. They speak to people at a certain time and in a certain place, which might have some similarity to our world but also have their own unique, historical constellations. They do not speak to the human race in general but are addressed to specific people in concrete, historical situations. The Bible only comes alive for us when we escape the letter of its words and hear what the Spirit is saying through it to our own specific circumstances of life. The circumstances in which we live our lives are filled with many issues that are not specifically addressed in the Bible—abortion, euthanasia, capitalism, communism, etc. The specific will that the Lord communicated to His people of old can only provide parameters by which we may test the spirits and discern His will in these matters but can never replace the Spirit, who relates His will to the believer personally and directly. While the will of God is consonant with what He revealed to His prophets and apostles, it is still unique and personal and contains God's special call to each of His children.[41]

Doubt is a necessary corollary to this concept of divine revelation. Divine revelation might be objective in itself, but there is always something lost when the Spirit transmits its truth to our soul. No one receives the transmission with certainty. Something is always lost when it is appropriated within. Conservative certainty can never dispel the doubts that remain—doubts that liberals inflame with their scientific cynicism—doubts that reason itself can never eliminate. We wonder whether God has truly spoken or whether we have understood His will in all its fullness, and so we waver in our convictions—at least those who confront their doubts and confess their sins. We waver like John the Baptist, who prepared the way for the Lord with his testimony and then wondered whether Jesus was the one or should he look for another (Matt. 11:3). The decision to believe or confess anything is given no guarantee. We can never be cocksure. We can never know where we stand (1 Cor. 10:11). No one can fathom the passions of the soul or the depths of the divine Word. Its expression is uttered with great risk. Its utterance must point beyond our own insufficiencies and bask in the light of the divine presence, which alone can fill our words and lives with meaning.

Even our belief in God can never be proven beyond all doubt. Reason could argue one way or the other but never resolve the issue in any definitive way. Faith is more a venture of the soul than a rational calculation reached at the end of a syllogism. It wants God to exist for existential needs, which resonate in the soul but not in the head. "To believe is to long for His existence." It is to hunger and thirst for righteousness. It is to have the courage to be or affirm the meaning of it all in the midst of so much darkness and despair. It is to crave for eternal happiness and hope for a life that can escape the oblivion of an eternal darkness. It cannot rationalize or justify its passion with sufficient reason, and it should not present a cover for what arises elsewhere—a disingenuous self-justification for what arises from the heart. "The heart has its reasons which reason does not understand." No defense can be mounted against those who wish to employ their reason and deprecate its longings—those like Feuerbach who say that religion is nothing but wishful thinking or those like Freud who say that we must grow up and renounce infantile, neurotic longings for protection from a divine father. Faith wants to believe too much to listen to these possibilities. It does not care so much about the contradictions of reason but prefers to embrace what gives it hope and vitality. It prefers Cicero, the Roman orator, who said that he would rather be wrong with those who affirm immortality than right with those who deny it. It prefers Peter, the disciple of Jesus, who remained steadfast with his Lord while others left the program complaining that the sayings of Jesus were much too difficult to accept. Peter did not know where else to go. Only Jesus "had the words of eternal life" (John 6:60, 66-68). Peter had no choice but to venture into the unknown and take that leap of faith, because the alternative was much too dark. For those who did not follow, they had their reasons, plenty of reasons, but none of them were sufficient to save their souls.[42]

Notes

1. G. Gallup, Jr. and S. Jones, *100 Questions and Answers: Religion in America* (Princeton: Princeton Research Center), 2, 70-71, 168-169, 175, 202, 206; G. Gallup, Jr. and J. Castelli, *The People's Religion: American Faith in the 90s* (New York: Macmillan Publishing Co., 1989), 29, 36, 47-48.

2. G. M. Marsden and B. J. Longfield, eds. *The Secularization of the Academy* (New York and Oxford: Oxford University Press, 1992), 3-4, 10-11, 55, 199; G. M. Marsden, *The Soul of the American University: From Protestant Establishment to Established Unbelief* (New York and Oxford: Oxford University Press, 1994), 4, 99; L. Versey, *The Emergence of the American University* (Chicago: University of Chicago Press, 1970), 26, 34, 48.

3. *Ibid.*, 3, 26, 47, 65; Marsden, *The Soul*, 4, 104-105, 254, 267, 365, 440.

4. Marsden, *The Soul*, 38-42.

5. *Washington Times* (April 21, 1994); R. L. Tafel, "And From My Lips Will Come What Is Right," *Harvard Magazine* (July/August, 1991), 21. As cited in T. C. Reeves, *The Empty Church: The Suicide of Liberal Christianity* (New York: The Free Press, 1996), 17.

6. A. L. Goldman, *The Search for God at Harvard* (New York: Random House, 1991), 43ff., 113, 117, 173-178, 247.

7. H. Cox, *The Secular City* (New York: Macmillan Publishing Co., 1966), 60ff., 217.

8. *Ibid.*, 2, 72-74, 119, 154.

9. *Ibid.*, 4, 99-100.

10. E. S. Fiorenza, *In Memory of Her: A Feminist Theological Reconstruction of Christian Origins* (New York: Crossroads), 4, 13, 18, 21-23, 30-33.

11. *Ibid.*, xiii-xiv.

12. D. D'Souza, *Illiberal Education: The Politics of Race and Sex on Campus* (New York: Vintage Books, 1992), 160-161, 239; T.

Sowell, *Inside American Education: The Decline, The Deceptions, The Dogmas* (New York: The Free Press, 1993), x, 176, 189ff., 210ff., 265, 345.

13. Marsden and Longfield, eds., *The Secularization*, 35-37, 210-216.

14. G. W. Ahlström, *The History of Ancient Palestine* (Minneapolis: Fortress Press, 1994), 327-338.

15. Celsus, *On the True Doctrine: A Discourse against the Christians*, trans. R. J. Hoffmann (New York and Oxford: Oxford University Press, 1987), 56, 118-119.

16. S. G. Cole, *The History of Fundamentalism* (Hamden and London: Archon Books, 1963), 251; N. F. Furniss, *The Fundamentalist Controversy, 1918-1931* (New Haven: Yale University Press, 1954), 56-57; R. Hofstadter, *Anti-intellectualism in American Life* (New York: Alfred A. Knopf, 1963), 133; N. Chomsky, *The Prosperous Few and the Restless Many* (Berkeley: Odonian Press, 1994), 78; *Secrets, Lies and Democracy* (Tucson: Odonian Press, 1994), 54-56; G. Marsden, *Fundamentalism and American Culture* (Oxford: University Press, 1980), 212.

17. Marsden, *The Soul of the American University*, 440.

18. F. Schleiermacher, *On Religion: Speeches to its Cultured Despisers*, transl. J. Oman (New York and San Francisco: Harper & Row, Publishers, 1958), 36, 124, 141, 180, 222-223, 241-243; *The Christian Faith*, ed. H. R. Mackintosh and J. S. Stewart (Philadelphia: Fortress Press, 1976), 46, 63, 181-182, 192, 144, 385.

19. J. Wellhausen, *Prolegomena to the History of Ancient Israel* (Gloucester, MA: Peter Smith, 1973), 1-2, 59, 71ff., 77ff., 103, 235, 293, 412, 423-424.

20. D. Strauss, *The Life of Jesus Critically Examined*, ed. P. C. Hodgson and G. Eliot (Philadelphia: Fortress Press, 1972), passim.

21. A. Schweitzer, *The Quest of the Historical Jesus*, trans. W. Montgomery (New York: Macmillan Publishing Co., Inc., 1975), 252, 307-316, 324-325, 350-351, 401-402.

22. M. Foucault, *Madness and Civilization: A History of Insanity in the Age of Reason*, trans. R. Howard (New York: Vintage Books, 1988), 12-15, 48, 57, 73, 225-228, 239, 251-253, 269; *Discipline & Punish: The Birth of the Prison*, trans. A. Sheridan (New York: Vintage Books, 1979), 27, 30, 194, 195; R. Visker, *Michel Foucault: Genealogy as Critique*, trans. C. Turner (London and New York: Verso), 9-10, 15, 18-22, 41, 100-101.

23. S. Fish, *Doing What Comes Naturally* (Durham and London: Duke University Press, 1989), 532, 536, 551-553; E. Showalter, *Hystories: Hysterical Epidemics and Modern Culture* (New York: Columbia University Press, 1997), 30-31, 41-42, 145-146.

24. T. S. Kuhn, *The Structure of the Scientific Revolution* (Chicago: University of Chicago Press, 1970), 2-7, 18, 23, 34, 96, 109, 112, 121-122, 137-138, 158, 166-170.

25. *Ibid.* 54-55. The early Wittgenstein, however, supplies some clues for escaping the absolute subjectivity of Fish and Kuhn. He believes that our language does express a logical picture, and this logic can depict the world. It is related to the logic that is inscribed in the state of affairs around us. It is through the correlation or relationship of elements in a picture that the picture touches reality. This is how we can recognize what is being depicted. This is how we keep from bumping our shins on the furniture. This is how we predict certain events in the future.

26. R. A. Spivey and D. M. Smith, *Anatomy of the New Testament* (Englewood Cliffs, NJ: Prentice Hall, 1995), 66-67, 97-98, 131, 164-165, 203-211, 237-238, 241, 249, 256.

27. Gallup and Castelli, *The People's Religion*, 17, 60-63; Gallup and Jones, *100 Questions and Answers*, xv, 2-9, 175, 184, 188.

28. *Ibid.*, 93, 265; Gallup and Jones, *100 Questions and Answers*, xv, 70-73, 101, 140, 176-178, 187.

29. R. Wuthnow, *The Struggle for America's Soul: Evangelicals, Liberals, and Secularism* (Grand Rapids: Wm. B. Eerdmans Publishing Co., 1989), 23, 164-167, 178, 183-184; S. L. Carter, *The Culture of Disbelief* (New York: Doubleday, 1993), 57; Marsden, *The Soul*, 4, 365, 440.

30. W. E. Hordern, *A Layman's Guide to Protestant Theology* (New York: Macmillan Publishing Co., 1968), 72.

31. J. S. Mill, *On Liberty and other writings*, ed. S. Collini (Cambridge: University Press, 1994), 41, 44, 48-50, 53-54.

32. *Ibid.*, 8, 67, 106.

33. A. de Tocqueville, *Democracy in America* (New York: A. Knopf, 1963), 1:260-267; 2:10-11.

34. T. C. Reeves, *The Empty Church*, 1, 10ff., 15, 29, 32; Gallup and Castelli, *The People's Religion*, 17, 135, 139; Gallup and Jones, *100 Questions and Answers*, 198ff.

35. J. G. Machen, *Christianity and Liberalism* (Grand Rapids: Wm. B. Eerdmans, 1977), 2, 50ff., 109, 160, 167.

36. S. Strehle, *The Catholic Roots of the Protestant Gospel: Encounter between the Middle Ages and the Reformation* (Leiden, New York, and Köln: E. J. Brill, 1995), 9-11.

37. *Ibid.*, 13-14, 61-64; P. Tillich, *The Courage to be* (New Haven and London: Yale University Press, 1980), 3, 34, 66, 177-180.

38. P. Tillich, *Systematic Theology* (Chicago: University Press, 1976), 3:44ff., 79, 342ff., 355.

39. G. Bahnsen, *Theonomy in Christian Ethics* (Nutly, NJ: The Craig Press, 1979), 13, 33-35, 112, 169-170, 217, 439, 445-447, 457; *By This Standard* (Tyler, TX: Institute for Christian Economics, 1985), 37, 52, 140-142, 277-278. It must be said that the temper of the later work is much more chastened than the former.

40. E. Brunner, *Justice and Social Order*, trans. M. Hottinger (New York and London: Harper Brothers, 1945), 99-103.

41. Cf. K. Barth, *Church Dogmatics*, III/4: 11, 31.

42. M. de Unamuno, *The Tragic Sense of Life in Men and Nations*, trans. A. Kerrigan (Princeton: University Press, 1977), 82-84, 132, 202-203; B. Pascal, *Pascal's Pensées*, trans. W. F. Trotter (New York: E. P. Dutton & Co., Inc., 1958), 78ff. (277ff.); S. Kierkegaard, *Concluding Unscientific Postscript*, trans. D. F. Swenson (Princeton: University Press, 1974), 33, 53-54, 96, 182; *Philo-*

sophical Fragments, trans. D. F. Swenson (Princeton: University Press, 1974), 79-81, 104-105; *Feath and Trembling and the Sickness unto Death,* trans. W. Lowrie (Princeton: University Press, 1974), 46.

CONCLUSION

The Power of the Spirit

The problems of a society can never find a solution through the enactment of more laws. Legalistic solutions from the left or the right do not touch the soul of a people or produce heartfelt conformance to what is intended. Loopholes are created. Ways are found to circumvent the intention. The spirit of the law is countered by legalistic devices, which conform to the letter of its words but avoid obedience to its message.

Take, for example, the problem of pornography in our society. One could draw lines and attempt to censor certain types of material, but this could never eliminate the omnipresence of its message when the spirit of a people has become so addicted to sexual stimulation. If the demand is there, academia will find the mystery of life in its forces, books will romanticize about its lusts, and the media will titillate the audience with graphic displays and "dirty" secrets. Laws might help to curtail some of its forms, but they can never prevent those who have set their mind in this direction from fulfilling their desires. Laws might even stimulate those desires with *forbidden* fruit and *illicit* behavior. They might even provide a pretext for rebelling against the

177

puritanical yoke of traditional taboos. Even if sex has become the noisiest of our preoccupations, many are convinced that we still need to be liberated from the past, come
out of the closet, and end our silence with a continuous,
uninhibited display of sexuality.[1]

It is the spirit of a people that provides the impetus for
its life. Laws cannot regenerate what comes deep from within.
Whatever made America great in the past is related more to
the religious and philosophical longings of its people than to
the special circumstance of its existence or the precise letter
of its laws. South America was conceived in the modern
world at the same time as our country. It lived in relative
isolation from foreign hostilities and was filled with plenti-
ful resources and fertile plains. Its countries even tried to
imitate the American Constitution and enact similar laws,
but without the same spirit it could never replicate the same
success. Its spirit was all-too-different. It preferred to blame
others for its shortcomings than search its own soul. It blamed
the countries in its region and conducted constant revolution to change unjust circumstances. It blamed America for
corrupting its social order and raping its natural resources.
But it could never replicate a spirit that works honestly with
its own hands, breathes life into its possessions, and creates
wondrous technological marvels. It could never find a use
for its oil without Yankee ingenuity and Puritan know-how.
Its land needed spirit to give it life.[2]

Of course, the history of America itself has much ambiguity. One could write a more cynical account of its history like Howard Zinn's *A People's History of the United
States* and emphasize the depravity of this nation with much
justification. Life after all is filled with ambiguity, and no
country has conducted itself in a manner worthy of divine
blessing. Even under the best of intentions political solutions involve a compromise between alternatives, the neglect
of valid claims, and the oppression of those left out. Its
wisdom is not divine, and its resources are limited. But
ultimately we must arise above the cynicism that would run

the country down into the pits of despair. We must look again through the eyes of faith toward the hope that God will mend our ways and use our works. We must look beyond our political system and its labyrinth of laws to the God who contains all power and can breathe life into dead works and dead letter.

There are no laws, written on tablets of stone, that one can read and enact and expect results. Even the Bible does not contain a specific political agenda or form of governance for us to follow and insure future success. No special offices are listed, no social order is prescribed, and no permanent structure is allowed to replace the work of the divine Spirit in its people. The Lord raises up His servants and affords His wisdom according to the need of each age. In the Old Testament, He prefers to raise up His own charismatic leaders instead of consecrating a self-perpetuating dynasty of royal privilege. When the children of Israel wanted to replace Samuel with a king and his family, it greatly displeased the Lord. He felt that they no longer wished to trust His ways or wait upon His Spirit to raise up the vessel of His own choosing. It brought judgment upon them in the form of what they wanted [(i.e., a dynasty of kings who would force them into royal service and increase their financial burden through taxes (1 Sam. 8)]. In the New Testament, the Lord's servants are found among those who are meek and lowly and have no political power whatsoever. It does not contain a political agenda or prescribe social laws to those who have no power. Christ establishes a church, which is to subsist as a nonpolitical, asocial force of His Spirit throughout the world. Its instructions are related to the conduct of individuals and their relationship within a fellowship, but are not explicitly intended to be applied to a societal context in any literal way. When Christ tells His followers to turn the other cheek, He is not overturning the societal laws of the Old Testament or demanding that all governments renounce the sword. His commandments are intended for those who wish to follow His will on a personal basis. When He tells

His disciples to renounce hatred and lust within the depths of their soul, it is only through the power of His Spirit that their hearts can find regeneration and cleansing.

A difficulty arises when one wishes to translate the message of Scripture into a societal message or speak of God's will outside of it in the world at large. The social laws of the Old Testament were written for a people long ago. The personal ethics of the New Testament were designed for a different purpose in its most precise intendment. To search for divine counsel outside the message is a tenuous practice and subject to the same obscurity with which God presents Himself in the realm of nature. The will of God is not so clear outside the church's own special commission, which is revealed to it in written form. Whatever His will might be in the world at large, it is subject to the dullness and darkness of our minds. One cannot speak with simple confidence when addressing the social, political, and economic spheres, because these matters are not the concern of special revelation and the light of general revelation does not shine so bright as to overcome our own insufficiencies in nature. While God has not abdicated His Lordship in these matters, and one should seek His will, no one can speak with the same confidence in those areas, which depend more upon our own human insight than upon what is available to us in Scripture. "The secret things belong to the Lord our God, but the things revealed belong to us and our children, that we may observe all the words of this law" (Deut. 29:29). One should not be too presumptuous in matters that remain unrevealed in Scripture and unclear to the most sagacious of us.

Besides, the marching orders of the church are found elsewhere. The institutions of this world can never convey through their powers and rules and regulations the true righteousness that comes from the divine Spirit. It is the proclamation of the Gospel that is central to the mission of the church, not temporal matters of ephemeral concern. Society, culture, and politics, even in their most noble and humane forms, can only pale in their claim to our devotion before the eternity that awaits us all (1 Cor. 9:25, 26; 2 Cor. 4:17, 18). Whatever status the church might find for itself in this world the fundamental concern is not to emancipate its people from slavery to the world's forces, but to urge the Lord's servants to be true servants indeed, even to the point of suffering oppression for the sake of the Gospel (1 Pet. 2:18, 1 Cor. 7:20-24).

The power of God is only displayed in the weakness of His subjects. It is not found in those who employ whatever means possible to secure adherence to their message. It is not found in tyrants, who venture to expand their kingdom and influence beyond its proper domain. It is not found in Satan, who covets raw power in itself and aspires to exalt himself unto a throne of almighty and grandiose proportion (Isa. 14:13, 14). It is not found in pure possibility, absolute power, and brute force.

The power of His Spirit works in the midst of those who display humility and weakness (Zech. 4:6, 2 Cor. 10:1; 12:9). These are the fruits of His Spirit. Its subjects are often lost in the great, high-flown annals of human history, but their impact is well-known to God. His Spirit elects those who are the second born, not the first (Rom. 9:6-12), the least in age and stature (1 Sam. 16:7, 11), the weakest of people (Deut. 7:1), the smallest of tribes (Mic. 5:1), the base, the weak, the foolish, and the poor (1 Cor. 1:26, Luke 6:20; 10:21, James 2:5). It uses servant girls to convey the message and lepers to feed the nation (2 Kings 5-7). Few of them are given titles of grandeur or respect for their service. Few of them sit on a throne in Samaria, preside over the Sanhedrin in Jerusalem, or teach in a seminary in Alexandria.

Their ministry is often performed behind closed doors. Jesus, in fact, advises His disciples not to serve God so as to be seen by men. The hypocrites who pray on the street corner for public consumption will receive their reward from the public, but His disciples are not to be like them. "When you pray go into your room and shut your door, so that you might pray to your Father who is unseen, and your Father who sees what is unseen will reward you" (Matt. 6:6).

It is this ministry that Paul commends to the church in regard to its civic duty. "First of all I urge that entreaties, prayers, petitions, and thanksgiving be made on behalf of all men, in behalf of kings and all who are in authority, in order that we may lead a peaceful and quiet life in godliness and holiness" (1 Tim. 2:1, 2). This ministry receives no accolades or honorifics. It is certainly left unnoticed by those who prefer the power-plays of big government. There is no reporter to record its performance and no means of quantifying its results. It might even seem to be trivial to those who prefer public recognition or other means to fight for their cause. But these other means often prevent the church from fulfilling its primary service and compromise the integrity of its mission, no matter how noble the cause. The church should never fight for its place in the spotlight through whatever temporal and worldly means available.[3]

The Spirit does not need to promote its cause through the heavy hand of legalistic devices and bureaucratic machinery. The Spirit is not pleased with those who prefer coercive forces to His free and charismatic ways. His yoke is free from the burden of a structural dynasty or a labyrinth of laws. His ways require a space in which He might recreate our own personal lives and communities in accordance with His will. Each generation must possess the freedom to hear His call and heed its own special election, commission, and injunction. The Spirit blows wherever, whenever, and however He wishes, creating all things ever anew and supplying all of His servants with special gifts for each unique age. The government, if anything, should respond by limiting its role and thus maximizing the freedom of the citizens in recreating their society. Its laws should be kept to a minimum and ever change with the dawning of each new age.

There is no greater means of quenching the Spirit than to revere with right-wing politics the wisdom of the past—a past that is dead and gone—and impose its precise conformation on the present. Whatever remains of value from the past is no longer applicable in its own right or free from the need to reevaluate and reinterpret its form. It must ever be made anew within a history that has moved on and a Spirit who breathes life into dead letter. History is not a static entity, which can be captured in timeless truth or cyclical traditions. Life marches on and its issues change along with it. A society that wishes to forge ahead with the movement of history cannot worship the dead letter of the past or become straightjacketed by its laws in the present. It must ever be open to what the Spirit is doing. It must ever be open to what the times and seasons dictate. It must ever search for fresh insight and renewed vitality and pray, *"Veni, Creator Spiritus"*—Come, Creator Spirit.

There is no greater form of religious tyranny than left-wing political machinery, which attempts to impose its totalitarian designs upon the citizenry and so depose the reign of the Spirit in their lives. Religious freedom is found by minimizing the size and scope of the state, not by pretending its laws are secular or neutral and contain no religious implications for us. One cannot separate the sacred and the secular, but one can maximize the freedom of the citizens and the role of the Spirit by allowing space for His power to operate in their lives.

Whatever made America great in its past cannot be attributed to its desire to be secular or live in autonomy away from the presence of God and devoid of His Spirit. It did not erect a wall to separate its sacred and secular life, as if it could live without God. It did not create one nation without God. It did not treat its religious leaders with contempt or its devout as second class citizens, so as to destroy the matrix from which it arose. These people had rights to participate in their culture and served as a necessary witness to its spiritual underpinnings. Benjamin Franklin, one of the wisest of our founding fathers, knew this, and he thought that it was essential to promote religion in the public arena. He considered it most contemptible to undermine the spiritual nature of the government and its people through secular and liberal cynicism.

> That wise Men have in all Ages thought Government necessary for the Good of Mankind; and, that wise Governments have always thought Religion necessary for the well ordering and well-being of Society, and accordingly have been ever careful to encourage and protect the Ministers of it, paying them the highest publick Honours, that their Doctrines might thereby meet with the greater Respect among the common People; And that if there were no Truth in Religion, or the Salvation of Men's Souls not worth regarding, yet, in consideration of the inestimable Service done to Mankind by the Clergy, as they are the Teachers and Supporters of Virtue and Morality, without which no society could long subsist, prudent Men should be very cautions how they say or write any thing that might bring them into Contempt, and thereby weaken their Hands and render their Labours ineffectual.[4]

Notes

1. M. Foucault, *The History of Sexuality*, trans. R. Hurley (New York: Vintage Books, 1990), 1:8, 18, 33, 158-159.

2. A. de Tocqueville, *Democracy in America*, 1:167, 231-232, 319-321; M. Novak, *The Spirit of Democratic Capitalism* (New York: Simon & Schuster, Inc., 1982), 103, 278-279, 300.

3. K. Barth, *Community, State, and Church: Three Essays*, intro. W. Herberg (Gloucester: Peter Smith, 1968), 136, 167.

4. B. Franklin, *Writings* (New York: The Library of America, 1987), 149.

Epilogue

On my last trip to Washington, I decided to visit, of all things, the Lincoln Memorial. This required a considerable act of faith for a Southerner (or maybe I should say, outright apostasy). All true Southerners know that Mr. Lincoln's war violated their Constitutional right to secede from the union. The war had little to do with slavery and much to do with the North's continued domination of the South.

This knowledge I brought to his shrine as I ascended the marble steps to the white, colonnaded temple, which housed the enormous idol to northern oppression. I looked up at Lincoln sitting on his throne, looking down at the plebes, self-assured, godlike in his resolution and righteous in his cause. It was difficult for me to swallow all this. I certainly did not pay much respect to the image.

I then turned to read some of the inscriptions on the walls around the temple. On the north wall the Gettysburg Address was inscribed in bold, capital letters. Its words were all-too-familiar to have much meaning. On the south wall his Second Inaugural Address was inscribed in like manner—a text that I had never considered with much depth in understanding Lincoln or his war.

I will not say that I experienced an epiphany that day, but I will say that this text helped to illuminate what became most essential in my mind. The text speaks of the specific issues that brought the war—preserving the union being its pretext and emancipating "the colored slaves" the emerging cause. But the most essential matter, which dominates the text, is what concerned many of our forefathers— whether they had fulfilled the will of God and whether their cause was just. The text is filled with allusions and citations from Scripture, and its concern is that divine counsel be sought and its will be done, regardless of the outcome. While Lincoln clearly defends his cause, what appears most essential from his manuscript is not the victory of union forces but the triumph of the will of God in this and other matters. He admits that his cause does not embody its Spirit wholly and completely. He says that both sides pray to the same God, and neither side has obtained an answer to their supplication in full. What is important is that neither side should judge one another and both sides should continue to seek a divine resolution to the conflict.

A new image of Lincoln emerged from my visit. It was not embodied in the idolatrous image, which dominated the temple, but found within a text, written by a man and filled with his spirit. It forced me to recall a more faithful image of the man, the last portrait taken of him before his death, so dark, so pitted, and so aged. Here I saw a face ravaged by war, tormented by his decision, and vexed with doubt. Perhaps, Mr. Lincoln was wrong to invade the South and the rebels had every right to leave the union, but one matter emerged above all this in the text and in the portrait—Lincoln had struggled in his conscience with the will of God throughout the war. Perhaps in the midst of his troubled decision, I thought, the God of all mercy could still bring to fruition His will through such a vessel. He could still make all things right if we sought His will and hoped that He would honor our efforts. It might be that the Spirit even works above and beyond the letter of our laws and the depravity of our deeds. In fact, it might be that bad laws and poor decisions serve His will better if they are made in a spirit of supplication than good laws without the love, truth, and beauty it takes to carry these laws to their fulfillment.[1]

Notes

1. Cf. Montesquieu, *The Spirit of the Laws*, 1.811ff. (119ff.).

We welcome comments from our readers. Feel free to write to us at the following address:

Editorial Department
Huntington House Publishers
P.O. Box 53788
Lafayette, LA 70505

or visit our website at:

www.huntingtonhousebooks.com

═══════════════

More Good Books from Huntington House Publishers & Prescott Press

The Coming Collision
Global Law vs. U.S. Liberties
by James L. Hirsen, Ph.D.

Are Americans' rights being abolished by International Bureaucrats? Global activists have wholeheartedly embraced environmental extremism, international governance, radical feminism, and New Age mysticism with the intention of spreading their philosophies worldwide by using the powerful weight of international law. Noted international and constitutional attorney James L. Hirsen says that a small group of international bureaucrats are devising and implementing a system of world governance that is beginning to adversely and irrevocably affect the lives of everyday Americans.

Paperback ISBN 1-56384-157-6
Hardcover ISBN 1-56384-163-0

Cloning of the American Mind
Eradicating Morality Through Education
by B. K. Eakman

Two-thirds of Americans don't care about honor and integrity in the White House. Why? What does Clinton's hair-splitting definitions have to do with the education establishment? Have we become a nation that can no longer judge between right and wrong?

"Parents who do not realize what a propaganda apparatus the public schools have become should read Cloning of the American Mind *by B. K. Eakman."*

—Thomas Sowell, *New York Post*
September 4, 1998

ISBN 1-56384-147-9

Patriots
Surviving the Coming Collapse
by James Wesley, Rawles

Patriots, a fast-paced novel by Y2K expert James Wesley, Rawles is more than a novel — it's a survival manual. Could you survive a total collapse of civilization - a modern Dark Ages? Would you be prepared for the economic collapse, the looting, riots, panic, and complete breakdown of our infrastructure?

"More than just a novel, this book is filled with tips on how to survive what we all hope isn't coming to America."
—Jefferson Adams, *The Idaho Observer*

ISBN 1-56384-155-X

Government by Decree
From President to Dictator
Through Executive Orders
by James L. Hirsen, Ph.D.

Could Americans lose their constitutional rights and be forced to live under martial law with the stroke of pen? Sound like fiction? Wrong! Right now, through the use of a tool called an executive order, the President of the United States has the power to institute broad, invasive measures that could directly impact the lives of average, everyday Americans. What might trigger the exercise of this type of awesome power? Any number of things could, but for certain, a crisis, real or manufactured, is the most frightening prospect.

ISBN 1-56384-166-5